*A*nne Hillman celebrates life through the sort of nature writing which descends into our inner recesses, not with the microscope of a Lewis Thomas or the atom smasher of the physicist but down and through prairie dog-like tunnels to discover feelings which stand under us, an architecture we never knew existed. Moreover, she is like Dante's Beatrice, a patient and beautiful tour guide...

Wes Jackson, Ph.D.
Geneticist, President, The Land Institute, Salina KS
author of *Alters of Unhewn Stone* and *Becoming Native to this Place* (1994)

In beautifully written prose, Anne Hillman shines a brilliant light on a new way of relating to our planet and each other...an important book that will help every reader meet the challenges and discover the joys of the new millenium.

Hal Zina Bennett, Ph.D.
author of *Follow Your Bliss*

In this time when the inner, subjective dimensions of psychic life are all but drowned out by our cultural obsession with objective knowledge, achievement and material fulfillment, Anne Hillman's *Dancing Animal Woman* is medicine for the soul. Her story shows us that there is a redemptive intelligence within each of us that restores our sense of personal wholeness and our connection to Life if we will but make the time to listen and honor its voice within us.

Richard Moss, M.D.
author of *The I That Is We, The Black Butterfly,* and *How Shall I Live?*

The Dancing Animal Woman

A Celebration of Life

For Louanne — with love and a wish for creative and fulfilling journey

Anne Hillman

Anne a Hillman

BRAMBLE ❖ BOOKS

Connecticut

The proceeds from the sale of this book will be
tithed by the author to ecologically oriented non-profit organizations.

For information write to:
Bramble Books, PO Box 209, Norfolk, Connecticut 06058

Library of Congress Cataloging-in-Publication Data

Hillman, Anne.
    The dancing animal woman : a celebration of life / Anne Hillman.
        p.   cm.
    ISBN 1-883647-01-0 (alk. paper) : $14.95
    1. Hillman, Anne. 2. Religious biography—United States. 3. Women and religion. 4.
Women—Religious life. I. Title.
BL73.H55A3 1994
200'.92—dc20
[B]   94-5695
                                                                              CIP

First Printing 1994
1 3 5 7 9 10 8 6 4 2

Printed in the United States of America

The paper used in this publication meets the minimum requirements of
American National Standard for Information Sciences—Permanence of Paper
for Printed Library Materials, ANSI Z39.48-1984.

Tempera painting for cover by Carole Peccorini.
Calligraphy for Figure 1 by Suzan P. Gray.
Pen and ink drawing for Figure 2 by Denise Hillman Moynahan.

Acknowledgments

When something new is being born—an idea, a book, a self—
it is very tender. It needs encouragement but it also needs to be
tempered by honest feedback. I offered my first poetry to Michael
and Noreen Scofield for professional review. If they had not
responded with such care to both requirements, I might not have
dared continue to show my writing to anyone but close friends and
family. Several others did the same. Barry Gill, a wise human
being and a gifted teacher, helped me to understand that finding
my voice was, indeed, finding my soul. He also understood how
crucial to any creative work was the ongoing support of peers, and
I have been blessed with the continuous wisdom and intelligence
of a writing group initially formed under his guidance. For five
years, Carole Peccorini, Pat Sullivan, Harriet Wright and I have
met every month to listen to one another's work. We have travelled up to two hours each way to meet in each others' homes: to
read, to understand, to critique, and above all to honor each
other's creativity. For their commitment, honesty and love, I am
deeply grateful.

Brian Swimme ended a graduate course with an amazingly
respectful request for a final paper: "You have heard my ideas, now
I want to hear yours. *What is your life question?* All right, now
answer it." My question was *"How shall we learn to live as one
among many?"* It would never have gone further, had he not

pressed me (with his own astonishing brand of empowerment and enthusiasm), to expand my ideas and write a book. He then followed through, on his own time, with critical appraisal of several chapters.

Everyone should be blessed with the kind of critical support I have enjoyed with Hal Zina Bennett. An extensively published author and publishing professional, he has supplied understanding and unwavering enthusiasm in addition to his creative, editorial judgment. Best of all, we have laughed a lot together! Publisher Larry Bramble's excitement about the book's content, combined with his design and production skills, has made the publishing process a delight. The breadth of cover artist, Carole Peccorini's creativity has been an inspiration for many years.

The support of my friends and my family has meant a great deal to me. I wish I could name them all but I shall single out three. I am grateful to my sister, Denise Hillman Moynahan, for her artistic interpretation of the Languages of the Cosmos model. My mother, Kathryn Hillman, put in countless hours of proofreading and offered suggestions for clarification which proved very helpful.

And then there is my husband: When I first met George, he mused aloud about the thrill it would be to assist someone who was writing a book. How he has assisted! He has done the marketing and cooked the meals when I was under deadline; he has provided skillful questioning which required me to hone my ideas; he has read each chapter as it was being developed; at the end, he read the whole book aloud to me so I could listen. And then, there is something about somebody loving you that makes all the difference.

For the two women who were my guides on the journey down:

Susan G. Beletsis

and

Helen Mitchell

with gratitude for their life experience, their compassion and their inspiration,

and for

Brian Swimme

who inspired the telling of this story and whose passion for the story of the universe gave it a home.

Contents

Foreword • *xv*
Brian Swimme

Preface • *xix*
Embodiment

Prologue • *1*
The Seed That Must Crack

~

Part One
A New Vision:
Living as Part of the Whole

1. *The Tarantula and the Bull* • *15*
A real-life allegory of descent in which two dark creatures
guard the entrance to a new vision of living as part of the whole.

2. *The Wisdom of the Dance* • *25*
The sweeping silhouette of a thousand starlings
reminds us of a mysterious wisdom.

Part Two
A Letting Go

3. The Briefcase in the Garden • 39
A personal turning point heralds the call to leave the path
of "reaching the top" and take a journey of descent instead.

4. Daring Not to Know • 47
Daring to step outside the language of words
and lose control of the world. (Language, Image)

5. Entering the Dark • 57
A descent into the body and the first of its many languages.
(Emotion, Feeling)

6. The Compass Bearer • 71
A strange compass with a spiral shell at the center and no needle
provides new bearings for transformation in the midst of chaos. (Figure 1)

Part Three
An Expanding Identity

7. Dance, Wild Beast • 91
Claiming the wild one brings physical, emotional and
ecological healing. (Sensing, Instinct)

8. Languages of the Cosmos • 109
Truth from a child's toy about the many ways
we learn wisdom. (The Shamanic, Dream) (Figure 2)

9. The Tender Connection • 137

Dissolving the boundaries of space and time—
the subtle meeting place between mind and nature. (Intuition)

10. The Cosmic Story • 149

A lyric narrative celebrates the unfolding cosmos as a sacred story
which excludes no one. (The Unfolding Story of the Cosmos)

Part Four
A Capacity to Care

11. Three Cosmic Births • 165

A shamanic journey shows three evolutionary births
and illuminates the birth into Care.

12. Integrity: The New Ecological Identity • 181

Integrity defined as the new and evolving human identity of belonging.

13. Hymn to the Mystery • 199

If Integrity is the figure, then Mystery is its ground,
the infinite unknown, a depth brimming with the constant
creativity of the universe. (Mystery—The Creative—The Void)

14. Coda: Belonging • 217

A chance encounter with a small boy on a beach.

Notes • 221

Foreword

What you hold in your hands is a rare and unusual book, one of the first of its kind. On one level, *The Dancing Animal Woman* documents a journey in consciousness as it takes place in the author over the course of her adult life; but on yet another level, this story of personal transformation is an explicit expression of a major shift in cultural awareness that, in varying degrees, involves every thinking person of our time. The shift is not only a personal transformation, not only a cultural change; it is, as Anne Hillman celebrates, a shift from one form of humanity to another.

Over the two million years of human existence, several funda-mentally distinct forms of human consciousness have been devel-oped. The most easily identifiable are the *animistic*, characterizing humans during the Paleolithic era; the *mythological*, a form com-mon during the beginnings of the Neolithic villages; the *classical*, which is the awareness out of which all the great civilizations of the planet arose; and the *modern*, that particular orientation that emerged simultaneously with the growth of technology and indus-trial society. Even with so rough a sketch of the evolution of consciousness, represented by this listing of four modes, we can begin to appreciate the full significance of Anne Hillman's work. *The Dancing Animal Woman* is a story of a woman's journey from one era of life into another—a new era of her personal journey; a new era of her culture's journey; but even more, a new era of our species's journey, one that brings us into a new human mode of consciousness.

What makes this transformation and *The Dancing Animal Woman* unique in the history of humanity is the level of conscious self-awareness brought to the work, for we have no evidence that previous peoples, as they moved from one form of consciousness to another, were aware that they were involved in such a major shift. For instance, though we have works of art that express the change taking place as some groups of humans moved from animistic to mythological consciousness, we have no artist who clearly expresses that she was aware not only that this shift was taking place within her, but that she herself was extending the transformation through her own creative work.

Anne Hillman is not only aware of the pervasive transformation gathering up humanity as we move into a new way of being in the universe, she is also aware that by giving an artistic form to her journey, she offers her serious readers the possibility of entering their own journeys in consciousness, journeys that can benefit from what Anne Hillman has come to know and feel. *The Dancing Animal Woman* is a book to be meditated upon. It is a book filled with fertile suggestions for anyone stunned by industrial society's destructive impasse, and interested in exploring ideas and practices that promise a more satisfying perspective on such central questions as the nature and role of the human species here at the start of a new millennium.

The fundamental conviction of *The Dancing Animal Woman* is that we live in a meaningful universe, one filled with voices. Our primary task is to become "receivers," people capable of responding to the many languages and voices surrounding and filling us. Through her struggles, her joys, her ordeals, and her pondering, Anne Hillman has learned to listen to these many voices, whether of the body, or the animals, or the image, or the haunting presence of the dream, or the ancient energy captured by the word. With *The Dancing Animal Woman*, she leads us into this practice of becoming receivers. She teaches by her example how we too can learn to respond to these many voices. And as we learn, we come to realize that, by her faithful practice of attending, Anne Hillman has learned not only how to listen, but also how to become one of the primal cosmological voices of our time.

Brian Swimme, Ph.D.

Director, Center for the Story of the Universe at the
California Institute of Integral Studies, San Francisco.
Co-author, with Thomas Berry, of *The Universe Story*,
author of *The Universe is a Green Dragon*.

Author's Preface

Embodiment

This is the story of a woman's journey to reclaim the lost passion of her body. It is not merely sexual passion, but a fire that animates one's entire being and sings to everything else that lives. Make no mistake about it: It is a story of incarnation—an incarnation of the passion and power of the universe. An embodiment of the wild soul.

It was her soul that was lost—lost in the long, long unfolding of a much larger story, a story that encompasses us all. For this is not merely a personal tale. *Rather it traverses the boundaries of space and of time, of individuals and species, creatures and cosmos.*

The Dancing Animal Woman is a celebration of life—*all of it.* It gathers up the skeins of love and grief, rage, the destructive, beauty and death, and weaves the story of a woman at the end of the twentieth century into the blazing story of the universe.

It is an adventure: an invitation to a vision of human nature and a quality of aliveness, found only in intimate relationship with our deepest selves and the whole community of life. That ecological community is a tapestry, but few writers have addressed the tangled threads of its underside—the necessary inner work to permit a human life to become integral with the earth. The book describes such an interior journey.

I did not know I was on a search for the passionate aliveness that I found. I only knew I was lonely and lost, and that something was drawing me deeper beneath the surface of my life in search of meaning. There is a hunger in people to touch those depths; to know that our lives are sacred; that our hearts are truly capable of love. It is a yearning to be all that we can be. A longing for what is real.

For me, it was like a nagging emptiness in my midsection. I think that hollowness often propels us on the spiritual journey, though at the time, I didn't know what a spiritual journey was. But as I entered adulthood, I began to ask with an urgency what that might be, of people whom I thought should know. I talked with ministers and teachers about God and death, and asked about ritual and parables. Again and again I circled the questions of meaning and purpose like a beast tracking its prey. I was stalking the real.

I brought books about philosophy and psychology home from the library, but what I found did not feed my soul. Instead, I was left dry and depleted by responses that had no relevance to the wonder and ecstasy and fierce exaltation that I knew in my bones had a kinship with holiness. Some ancient memory of silence and mystery stirred in me still, and had been laid bare in fragile moments of beauty and firelight and acts of love. But these religious and psychological frameworks offered me coded interpretations, theories and metaphors which never *met me*.

How I yearned for that kind of meeting! I didn't know at the time that my questions and yearning alone were the barest of beginnings. Then life itself took charge. *Life either throws you on the spiritual journey or it does not.* As the events which unfolded over a decade threw my life into disarray, I realized that no reading or study could have prepared me, no answers paved the way.

The spiritual journey is a *creative* journey. It's about birth. It calls us past the boundaries of convention. It tests our willingness to see life in a new way and our courage to express it: for new ways of viewing life fly in the face of what is commonly accepted. We become new, and in this ongoing birthing, we bring new forms to life as well. Life itself has become a creative act, full of vitality and richness and passion.

When life challenged me to this kind of radical change, I had to learn a new way of living, step by step. As I entered into that bewildering process of experiment and discovery that I now call the spiritual journey, I longed most of all for confirmation from others who had been on similar paths. I wanted to hear from them about their experiences. For one thing, I was experiencing power-ful *bodily* sensations, but most writers weren't talking about that. In fact, very few writers shared much at all about their personal lives. Most removed themselves to a comfortable professional distance and spoke as authorities.

I could not relate the physical signals coming from my awaken-ing body to their clinical anecdotes and interpretations of ancient myths. I needed peers on this voyage, people who would express what went on *inside* them, who spoke to me from their hearts. I needed people who would encourage me by telling their stories, but who would not impose their views on me. When it came time to write about my own experience, I decided to write in a way that would offer that kind of empowerment and encouragement to others.

I wanted my words to be an open window to my soul; to find a voice which expressed both intellect and feeling, which acknowledged both body and spirit. I needed to express ideas, yet ground them in human experiences we *all* know intimately—a depth of feeling, bodily sensation and the beckoning of the soul—in languages of color and image, of dreams and particularly of energy. All these are languages of the body, for the spiritual journey as we humans know it is quite literally incarnate. It entails a descent into bone and tissue, thence to claim our creaturehood and our wisdom.

I experience the spiritual journey as a sacred journey of healing—of mind, heart, body and soul. But how could I speak of it? If I were to write in a purely logical fashion, whole selves that are me would go unhonored—the artist, the intuitive, the one called by mystery, the one who experiences life on many levels. If I were to write more intimately—poetry or a woman's journal—I would have to leave out the ideas which were so important to me.

Could I speak from my heart and honor my intellect at the same time? Could I hone the poetry of life's lessons and shape it to express what I felt and thought? I knew that if I could find a way to integrate those aspects of myself in one art form, I would feel I was being true to myself.

I was inspired by a poem:

> Take your practised powers and stretch them out
> until they span the chasm between two
> contradictions...For the god
> wants to know himself in you.[1]

My mind didn't understand the poem at all; yet it spoke to a depth in me that did, and said "follow it." At first, I simply couldn't find the words, so I began with a slide presentation using art, photography and linguistics.* Then I wrote a paper about my ideas. A friend who was an editor told me my writing was "marmoreal." I had to look the word up: it meant *"dense, like marble."* It wasn't a compliment! I practised writing for ten years— short narratives that I hoped would help me find a voice that was my own.

Finding my voice was finding my soul.

This is also the story of how my soul found me, and it was a wild soul. I wasn't prepared for how wild it was. This soul speaks different languages than I. I'm used to thinking in sentences and paragraphs and she speaks in colors and sensations I don't have a name for. Indeed, the greatest challenge of the journey entailed learning how to be receptive to her messages. These promptings were not disembodied channelings; they were grounded in my flesh.

It is her presence, *there*, that provides the missing link. It is *there* in the unity of passion and utter stillness that the spirit gazes out of our soft wild eyes. Thus embodied, we look around and discover that we are no longer lonely. We belong. Like running a finger along the single edge of a Moebius strip, we see that inside has become outside, and outside has turned inward. We have found the tender connection between our own lives and all that is. For the spiritual journey ultimately leads to something larger than self—to the eternal, to all of life, and more tangibly, to the earth. Throughout the book, the earth is given a voice—through moist

---

* Given at the National Meeting of the Organizational Development Network, Snowmass, CO, 1979.

sand and warm air currents, through granite and birds of prey, deer and iris, butterflies and tarantulas.

Morris Berman ends his recent book by saying:

> *Something obvious keeps eluding our civilization,*
> *something that involves a reciprocal relationship be-*
> *tween nature and psyche...*[2]

The Dancing Animal Woman begins where Berman leaves off. You will know the place, for this is your story, too. Though the details may be different, if you said yes to Life when it threw you on the journey, you have already embarked on the adventure. *We all know this place, for we are the journey. The Dancing Animal Woman* is an invitation not only to my journey, but to your own— and to the primordial and timeless soul that lives within you. My hope is that through this book, you will find your own experience confirmed and your own creativity encouraged.

Anne Hillman

Prologue

The Seed That Must Crack

The seed that is to grow
must lose itself as seed;
And they that creep
may graduate through
chrysalis to wings.

Wilt thou then, O mortal,
cling to husks which
falsely seem to you
the self?
                    —Wu Ming Fu[1]

Since the beginnings of time, life has cracked its seeds wide open so that something new might spill forth. In its slow experi-

1

mentation over the millennia, each and every form has been grist
for its mill: plant, animal, artistic idea, belief, cultural institution,
humanity itself. This is how life is; but we have resisted the crack-
ing of the seed. We've tried to hold onto forms as they are and not
let them break open with new creativity.

Yet life seems to be addressing us in the last days of the twentieth century, with an insistence that calls us beyond the forms we
know: the urgencies of jobs and family, the quest for liberation, the
social and economic complexities of our world.

Life calls us deeper. It calls us past our thoughts, our intellectual achievements; past our emotions and social relationships. One
by one and as a human species, *it calls us past who we think we are*.

It did not call me all at once to take that long, sacred journey
to find my wild soul. It was a slow shattering. Many seasons were
required to crack the seed. Like many of us, I spent the first decade
of my adulthood thinking I was in charge of my own life. I didn't
recognize that life itself had been in charge from the beginning.
But even as it threw me onto the path repeatedly, I ultimately lost
my way. One by one, life smashed my icons. And yet the smashing
was part of finding my way.

I would never have found the dancing animal woman, her
presence, her gifts of vitality and inner power, if I had not answered that deep inner call of life. Perhaps none of us would
answer—would leave these things we know to venture into the
unknown—without crisis. And it was the first crisis that began to
crack me open, as seed:

～

Prologue

On a crisp October night in New Hampshire many years ago, I
sat in a one-room wooden terminal building at a small airport
ringed with mountains and waited for the plane from Boston. My
seven year old daughter sat with me and my son, three and impa-
tient, tugged at me from the aisle as he crowed "Daddy coming
home! Daddy coming!" The plane was an hour late, and we
watched the moon peek in and out of the low clouds as the minutes ticked by on the clock on the opposite wall.

A small group waited for the five o'clock flight: two mothers
with babies, a student wearing a heavy athletic sweater from the
college where my husband taught (*probably a freshman meeting his
date for the big weekend, I thought*), an older couple, a man alone,
and a few women, one with a little girl about two. The toddler was
bored, and wandered aimlessly down the narrow aisle between the
wooden folding chairs. She tripped, then, gathering herself, sol-
emnly walked over to the student and laid her limp rag doll face
up on his knee. He blushed, trying to look manly, and we all
smiled, knowing how he felt. The loudspeaker crackled then, and
a pilot's voice announced the flight number of the plane we
awaited and continued, "Turning base for runway two-five."

After that there was silence. We waited. The plane didn't land.
I asked at the counter. No one seemed to know. I went to the
phone booth outdoors and called my teen-age baby-sitter. "Ellen,
would you run across the street and turn off our dinner in the
electric fry pan? Milton's plane is really late."

"Is that the plane from Boston?" she asked.

"Yes," I replied.

"We just heard it on the radio. It crashed on Moose Mountain."

3

~

It was end of the world. And the beginning of my search. My husband's life had vanished. One minute he was there. Another, he was gone. It was 1968 and I was just thirty three. In my solitude, the questions began. Two years before, with my focus on home, children and part-time teaching, I had written a friend, "Is this all?" Now, through Milton's death, I was thrust into the eye of life. *Life* mattered. I wanted to live and to live my life with meaning.

The safe future promised me in the fifties was gone. How would I manage with two small children? Where would we live? My sense of self was shattered. Who was I, if not my husband's wife with all that entailed in our small college town? Would I ever again feel I belonged? On what could I rely for my decisions? If I had only one life, how to live it? What, in fact, was real?

Quite unprepared for the culture shock, I left our community and moved to Cambridge, Mass., not knowing what I would do, though something in the racial and cultural collisions of the city called me. As I had been trained in the fifties, my former life had centered on my husband and his needs. In the ten years we had lived in a small college town, I had focused on a life of stability, security. The roles I carved out in relation to family, friends, community and college provided me a clear identity. That identity seemed to me almost as tangible as the protective mountains which surrounded the town like castle walls. Now my focus was change. Working, going to school, raising two small children, learning to date in an entirely different moral system, I tumbled into the currents and the liberation movements of the sixties. It was chaotic.

Prologue

I studied to become a consultant to organizations—a change agent. I attempted to help work groups increase their ability to function together; to assist them in developing a sense of community responsive to both the organization's and people's needs.

It was exciting for me, who once could make dinner table conversation about academic affairs but was barred from participating in them, to develop professional competence in a man's world. Still, these men seemed so sure of themselves, and I was constantly afraid. It was high risk work. As a woman in our culture growing up in the '40's and '50's, I had been raised to be protected, not to take risks. I remember joking with friends that the biggest risk I had taken before moving to the city was the decision of what to put in the market basket for dinner. A slight exaggeration, perhaps, but the difference between that and confronting the president of an organization was considerable! Mostly, the risks for those of us women who were "out there" in the business world in the late '60's and early '70's were the great unknowns. We were entering an entirely new environment, one for which we were not prepared.

There was no language yet for the kinds of things I experienced in my places of work. No one had named "sexual harassment," "the spotlight phenomenon," "fear of success." There were no models, no mentors. Loneliness, tension and pressure carved their watermarks in me as I learned to do three and four things at once. I was exhausted. At night, weary to the bone, I would try to shed the day's turmoil and attempt to fill the shoes of mother and father for a son and daughter anxious to tell me of their lives, and to be with me.

I had no idea how to be with myself.

Ten years passed. In those ten years we had lived in five homes and three states, the last, clear across the country to California, called this time by a freedom intuited rather than understood. Despite the hopes and effort I had invested in my children and friendships, in therapy, in religion and in a successful career, my life questions were still unanswered. I did not know who I was any more. I was lonely. And I certainly didn't feel I belonged. Behind me were several sets of friends, my family, my history and the clear-cut view of the world I had learned in the New England culture which had formed me.

By now, however, those descriptions of reality were shredding at the seams. It was not only my personal world which was rocked. Our entire generation had been shaken. The sixties and the post-Viet Nam years had cracked all the social foundations which had once offered us stability in our lives. We kept trying to hold onto the old beliefs and values as best we could, patching up our identities, marriages, churches, communities, patriotism, faiths, organizations, schools, beliefs. It was like trying to manage an assembly line for repairing an endless stream of cracked Humpty Dumpties. And I cracked.

Like many women who entered non-traditional work in the first fifteen years of the women's movement, my solutions to the conflicting set of demands (inside and out), did not work. Instead, they shattered me. Raised with an expectation of how to behave with men, my professional stance warred inside me with the need to please the board chairmen and company officers who were my clients. Confused about how to be female without attracting sexual advances, I shed my sexuality at the company's door. I was angry at being asked to serve cake and coffee at executive staff meetings because I was the only woman present. I felt guilty about

not finding another father for my children, and tried unsuccess-
fully to be two parents at once. I had bought the goal-oriented,
productive and successful cultural model for the workplace. And I
had lost my self: my body and my soul.

Broken by my own solutions, I learned I had to start all over to
find out who I was.

~

Many years later, after almost two decades of immersion in
organizations, remarried, my children grown, I found myself in
Egypt for the first time. Coming out of a tomb in the Valley of the
Dead into the bright sunlight, I was struck by the dark figure of a
woman passing by on the dusty road. She was tall, stately, wrapped
from her head to her ankles in a loose, dark brown robe. The
impression she gave was that of a moving pyramid of heavily
draped fabric swaying gently as if suspended from a string. She was
graceful, purposeful. Her hands hung simply at her sides. On her
head she balanced a huge water jug at an angle.

She was grounded. Sure of herself. She knew who she was. I
imagined her having learned from her mother and all the women
before her how to be a woman in that unchanging desert world.
Generations of women had probably walked the same path to the
well with much the same kind of jug—their young daughters
watching them carefully to see how it was done.

I longed to run up to her. To catch her hand and talk. She had
something I wanted desperately—a rootedness in who she was: in
her body, her culture, her history. She seemed as clear in her
identity as I was confused in mine.

~

Our two paths, mine and the Egyptian woman's, crossed at a time of millennial change and expectation throughout the world. On the one hand, there are many like me who look to new ways of being and new cultural forms with hope. At the same time, I long for a sense of belonging, of taking a part in a tradition and culture and community that reflects who I am and what my life is about.

At times I shun anything conservative, see it as a social or political "backlash." And yet there are other times when I recognize my own deep roots of conservatism and then I get in touch with something larger than political or religious movements. I have come to accept that conservative part of me; it is she who looks back over her shoulder at the woman carrying water. While I concede that there is no going back, my conservative self longs for simplicity, a way of life connected to the earth, *grounded*. For years in Cambridge and California I harbored a secret wish to return to that small New Hampshire college town where everyone knew me, and I knew who I was. The comfort of a small, rural community had been bred in me as a youngster growing up in a Vermont farm town, and I never lost that palpable sense of place, connectedness and belonging. Other times I imagined marriage to be the safe place to which I might return. Most difficult has been letting go of my old definition of womanhood, and with it the hope of recapturing the seeming certainty and clarity that my earlier forms of self definition once provided.

It has been hard for me to admit to myself on a deep emotional level that the old forms are gone forever. While my intellect has accepted change, my heritage and deeper dreams resist: Reality for *all* of us—men and women—is profoundly changed. We have *all* been thrust into a new environment for which we are not prepared. The majority of women with young children work. Only a minority of households are nuclear families. Urban sprawl and suburban living belie the dream of community we once knew. Extended families and lifelong local friendships are rare. Marriages fracture under the burdens placed on a single partner, innumerable human needs that were once met by an extended kinship. Social structures that once buttressed Western culture have buckled under the strain: the economy, religion, government, politics, education, family, personal values are all in flux. We are adrift in a culture that has broken loose of its moorings.

Now, with the environmental crisis, the stakes have moved higher. Our air, earth and water are being poisoned. Forests fall. Species disappear. The survival of our own species and the planet that has been our home are both profoundly threatened. Against the darkness of that new reality our search for guidance, for a sense of belonging and for roots is intensified.

～

When I was growing up, having roots meant being settled. It meant having a concrete sense of *place*. But this period approaching the year 2000 is a chaotic time. It is not stable. It is millennial. With the ground of familiar forms and place being plowed up beneath me, I had to find new soil in which to sink my roots. I needed to learn how to live *rooted in change*. It is a difficult task, one that most of us struggle with, though not all of us do so in any conscious way. In order to live rooted in change, we have had to learn to let go. For me, it has been hard to learn to free myself from my natural tendency to seek security—to cling. Nonetheless, along with so many others like myself, I have begun to stop seeking those "safe harbors" of the past, letting go of each static form, each arbitrarily defined reality, one by one. Old identities. Old dreams. Old hopes. Old self-images. People.

After a lifetime of focusing on the external world, my healing has been inward. Along with countless others I have come to accept that if we want to live lives of meaning, then *we have to do the inner work.* As my own path leads me in this direction, I have learned just how alive my body is. I have also discovered that it is receptive to many kinds of languages other than words. Many of us in Western culture have lost touch with the ways human beings once tapped into a fundamental wisdom buried deep in our genetic structure. Our *inner receptivity to life itself* has been dulled.

Along with that aliveness, my experience of the *context* for my life has radically changed. I have come to see that we are truly in and of an evolutionary process whose ends we cannot even imagine. Our reality is *process. An ongoing creation.* To live in that reality, in life, I have had to learn a new way of being grounded, one that the Egyptian woman carrying water doesn't know. I have sought depth in many places and found it in the moment, in feelings, in the simplest of experiences and in myself. I find it in my body. In the earth. In history.

In mystery.

The following pages tell the story of where that search for roots and depth and identity have taken me. As my experiences have unfolded one into the other, I've discovered something that I'd subtly known all along. It has to do with a connectedness that is currently attributed to the feminine. But what I am describing goes far beyond gender, mythology or sociology; in my journey I found the story of the universe and that story has dissolved all my old boundaries. It has seeped through my pores, has become a living part of me. As I claim all of the universe within me, I recognize my communion with all of creation. And as I take my place as one among many in that majestic story, I know that I belong.

≈

We stand at the turning point. At the same time we yearn to belong, the old social structures which once gave us a sense of membership are crumbling. At the same time we search for meaning, the cultural containers of political, social and religious beliefs (and I include here science and technology), prove too small to address the personal, cultural and planetary upheavals we are facing. Even as we attempt to ground our identities in locality or family or race or nationality or work, these identities fail; for they are identities based on exclusion, identities which keep others out, and they are not large enough to reach across the barriers of difference they perpetuate.

The seed has cracked. We have lost our identity.

I believe our task is broader than the definition of what it is to be a male or female in today's world. We are searching for *what it means to be human beings* in this great cosmic unfolding of which we are a part. The yearning is in all of us: To belong. To trust. To know what is real. Underneath the busy activities of our days we are silently seeking guidance for our decisions. Meaning. Depth.

I believe that what we are seeking is a wisdom that comes in the form of a *bodily experience*. It is a wisdom that exists in all of life. It is here that we will find guidance and meaning for the crucial years ahead for our planet. And that is what this book is about. It is an exploration of what it means to be a human being who belongs to a universe that is alive.

Part One

~

A New Vision:
Living as Part
of the Whole

1

The Tarantula and the Bull

Once in a while, perhaps only once in a lifetime, we are each given a glimpse of eternity. If only for a moment, the lens through which we view our world is wiped clean, and we are offered a vision to sustain a lifetime:

~

Dipping deep into the bends of the road, my new husband's motorcycle snaked down the dark side of Mt. Hamilton in the direction of the high Sierra. It was two years since I had first climbed onto the back of that once fearsome machine, and I had long since stopped holding on. My arms hanging loose, I let myself fall from side to side, my whole body leaning into the inner edge of the steep curves as I once had on the single blade of an ice skate (*holding the wide arc of a figure 8—what a dance!—the growing delight of living on first one edge, then the other, suspended, balanced as the weight shifts continuously under me, rolling like the surf.)*

We had driven straight up the Bay side of the mountain, climbing out of a grid of streets crowded with tightly packed buildings toward the peak where live oaks bulged out of broad, sloping fields, pungent with new-mown hay. The road became narrower and steeper as we got close to the top. "I love these curves, don't you?" "Too tight!" George shouted over the noise of the engine, "Makes me have to rein it in too much!" "Oh," I replied, settling back, understanding a little more of this stranger whom I loved. In my mind I'd thought he loved the sensuous curves in the same way I did. I hadn't realized the importance to him of the machine's sheer power—the feel of almost exploding into the landscape.

Descending the far side, the mountain showed us an entirely different face. It was darker, less traveled. As we made our way from switchback to hairpin turn, I exclaimed with surprise at the number of mountain ranges ahead of us. I think that was the closest I came to feeling any dismay at the terrain we had yet to cross; for a less familiar part of my mind had already begun to take charge, and I leaned back and listened. *"We don't really have a destination. If we get tired, we can always stop short of the foothills and sleep in the valley. Why not just see what happens?"* The idea enchanted me, pulling me away from my plans and certainties. It lured me further. *"You know, if I didn't have some idea of how the day was going to be, I could just relax and enjoy whatever came up!"* The voice was subtle, offering a possibility like a piece of chocolate cake on a round crystal platter. Delectable. *Simply open myself to all possibilities.* Something inside spread out slowly like the petals of a camellia. I was open. Unbounded. Willing to be surprised. And I was.

Half way down the mountain George stopped the cycle abruptly. "Look!" he shouted, pointing down at the road by his right foot. There, the size of my fist, was an enormous, spider-like insect. "It's a tarantula!" He was excited. The creature paused in its travels across the road, black and bristling, its large oval body suspended like a trampoline over eight hairy bent legs. We stood alongside it, two adults balancing a large machine, in respectful encounter with a powerful being in its own right. The three of us were immobilized, having a stare contest.

My mind raced to remember what I had heard about tarantulas. "*Poison,*" "*avoid,*" *and* "*tarantella, a seventeenth century dance movement!*" Then, "*I wonder if tarantulas can jump?*" I had just noticed my foot, resting on the motorcycle's peg, was not that far from the spider's head. In one moment, I felt fascination laced with terror, a sense of respect and a desire to protect it. I identified with it—as another creature.

We lingered for some time. As we drove off, I looked back over my shoulder to see the dark form ambling on its slow journey across the road. George began playing, weaving a ribbon candy path on the empty road, slanting deeper and deeper into the landscape.

> *What a liquid way to move on a road! To dance with its curves in a way no car can, so close to a fall—or a death—where the living happens. Unenclosed, all the smells of the world are here for the sniffing—cut hay and damp eucalyptus leaves, onions, marsh land, horse manure. Layers of air strike my face and my body, pockets of cold down at the foot of the hills; higher up, warm, moist currents brushing my cheeks. I look up*

17

*and see a hawk lazily glide along the updraft of warm
air above me, then slide down the edge of it—and I
wonder, is he laughing as he plays?*

We passed a sign: "Open Range," along the dry river bed. No
fences. No boundaries.

*Kind of like the way I am happening today. Freer, yet
more exposed. More vulnerable than in a car. Instead
of noticing the cars that pass, I look harder at the people
inside. I'm at their mercy. Boundaries make for some
measure of safety (whether they're steel capsules or
certainty about my destination), but they close me off,
too.*

Just as the hilly terrain began to level out, we came around a
corner and confronted a huge black bull challenging us from the
middle of the road. We stopped. I held my breath as he stared at us
unblinking, his powerful chest muscles glistening in the sun. We
stared back, as we had with the tarantula, guarded. The bull pawed
the ground. Minutes later he turned slowly and moved away. My
shoulders came down.

*Both of these dark creatures seem symbolic to me—like
ominous keepers of the gate in myth. They remind me
of those fearsome animals which stand at the entrance
to the underworld—or at the opening to the castle.
Dragons or dogs or many-headed beasts, they must be
greeted and ritually engaged in order to negotiate the
dangerous passage in search of the treasure or reward.*

I was beginning to let go again, my body an extension of the machine, rocking slowly from side to side. Then something extraordinary happened:

On the back of the motorcycle, I couldn't look straight ahead because George's helmet was directly in front of my face. So instead of watching the road, I looked to the side, seeing one scene after another slide past and disappear. Nothing remained but a constantly changing immediacy with no framework to hold my focus. It was a lot like sitting in the back seat of a car as a child, the front seats too high to see over, someone else in charge and an unfamiliar view whishing past the side window, cold and damp against my forehead.

During that autumn journey, orchard after orchard materialized and vanished. Long rows of trees converged on distant points: brown trunks in parade formation bearing walnuts, apricots and pears. I was lulled by the rumbling motor, the shifting temperatures and smells, and the strobing effect of endless patterns of tree trunks in the orchards. Part way across the valley, I realized that my perspective had radically shifted.

> *It's like I'm a child again. Not like returning to my own childhood. No. I feel like a child of the species! I know I am a part of all that has ever happened and everything that exists now. I'm woven into the whole fabric of things. I belong.*

It was an immediate, almost tangible insight. Everything in my world view had changed, yet how it had happened was unclear. I began to unravel my way back through the day the same way I back through a dream, trying to remember it. Now I was excited. Gesturing to George, I groped for a way to express what I'd just

19

experienced: "I need to stop a minute. It's something important. I'd like to talk." George slowed down and pulled over to the side of the road. We sat on the ground in a walnut orchard. After describing what had happened to me as best I could, I sought to give form to the current of excitement flowing through me:

"I wonder if it has to do with how we use our minds? I can't help but think about the beginning, when humankind was emerging and words suddenly became available. They must have had an extraordinary fascination. What a wonder to be able to communicate with one another! What control! Words gave us a way to deal with our fears of the unknown, just by naming them. We could label our experiences, categorize and evaluate them. What power! Power to bind and define. Power to *know*.

"But suppose we've got it all wrong? Suppose we got in the habit of seeing ourselves only as namers, makers and doers? Problem-solvers. Have we gotten mired down, exploring only those facets—namers, makers and doers—of our capacities for thousands of years at the expense of others? Maybe we have it backwards! What if there's another kind of knowing that's more important now? Something beyond control and explanation? What if the 95 percent of the brain that we supposedly don't use is just waiting for us to realize what we *really* are: not just movers and shakers. Not only figurer-outers and make-it-all-happeners—

"But *receivers. Living, breathing receivers!*"

Receivers. That was the word I needed! Now I remembered what had happened to me. Moments earlier, I had enacted how I felt that day: spreading out my arms as I rode on the back of the motorcycle, I became a wide "dish," an antenna stretched out to the fields and meadows, open to the sky, open to the hidden presence of the stars and planets behind the daylight—a receiver! And everything had changed.

My mind raced with brand new questions: "What if we completely changed our view of ourselves? What if, by becoming open, unbounded, receptive, we might access something more essential? Suppose we all came into the world able to comprehend things in wholes, experienced life in context, didn't slice things up? Then, as we learned language and imitated a human world view built over thousands of years, we began to see things as bounded and separate; to split things into opposites so they could be labelled and evaluated. Then when we went to school, we dissected reality even further. I know these skills are necessary. But this day tells me that something terribly important is missing.

"Suppose the capacity to see all sides, not be puzzled by paradox, was already there—that we could be simultaneously present to differences and opposites? *If that were so, then, I would just need to rest from my thinking and evaluating in order to hear. I might be more receptive to what is real.*"

I stopped, breathless, dazzled with possibility. As the years have passed, I've realized that on that day I had indeed caught a glimpse of reality. A glimpse of *Integrity*.

Common usage has disembodied the word "integrity" and made it safe; stripped it of sinew, bleached it to a bland code of ethics in business or boy scouts. Integrity is often defined as a moral stance, a subscription to certain publicly held values, an attempt to be loyal to one's friends, trustworthy in work. This usage is a pale shadow of its root meaning and real significance:

> *Integrity, n. (Latin.* **integritas,** *wholeness, soundness, from* **integer,** *untouched, whole, entire). 1. the quality*

or state of being complete; wholeness; entireness;
unbroken state. 2. the entire, unimpaired state or
quality of anything; perfect condition; soundness. 3. the
quality or state of being of sound moral principle;
uprightness, honesty, and sincerity.[1]

Integrity can be used to describe the unbroken quality of life in all its dimensions. This interwoven nature of reality is reflected in a sense of self which embodies all of creation: a living tapestry of creatures and cosmos, inside and outside, logic, imagination, mystery. Such an identity redefines what it means to be human.

To seek Integrity at this moment in history depends upon the embrace of much in ourselves that has been ignored and above all on honesty. It entails the courage to descend into our own bodies so that we learn who we really are from the bone and tissue we inhabit. For there is a wrong side to every tapestry. A woman who weaves knows that wrong side intimately. She has worked with the tangled threads, tied knots and embedded countless loose ends beneath the smoother surface. Integrity includes that dark, bodily dimension of reality, for therein lie both wisdom and vitality—a radiant leaping of life.

The interwoven nature of the entire experience on the motor-cycle is itself an example of Integrity. All the aspects of the day— the relatedness between persons; between what was going on inside and outside; between humans and a motorcycle and other creatures; between instinct, intuition and awe—are examples of the gathering up and weaving together of the shimmering threads of reality as it presents itself *all the time.*

In reflection, it has occurred to me that the day itself was an allegory. An actual experience, it nonetheless symbolized much of what followed on my life journey over the next ten years. The symbols of descent, of trusting the edge and of balance; of daring the dance between opposites; of not knowing and receptivity; of the dark creatures guarding the way to the unknown; the loss of familiar bearings and the risk of new ones; the emergence of creativity out of the loss of control—all of these actually unfolded in time. Even my attempt to express my experience that day is playing itself out now, as I write. The many-layered experience of the day and the discoveries in the years which follow might also be seen as an interweaving of *time*. Not only past and present were represented but future was symbolized as well. The day was like light glinting off one facet of a jewel—a brief flash which became more luminous as other facets subsequently revealed themselves in daylight and in dreams.

Integrity is the utterance of the universe, calling us out of our loneliness and isolation to depths within ourselves we have not dared. The promise of Integrity hints at our bereavement. It gives us a premonition of a deeper, more encompassing reality. Integrity is not an achievement, but a gift. It cannot be taught, but it can be embodied. One cannot be exhorted to Integrity but the hard choices for truth ease its emergence. Integrity calls us to creative fulfillment but that fullness comes out of a void.

There is a yearning in us for this reality. It waits like a staring cat, lies unblinking just beneath the surface as we occupy ourselves with our daily tasks. It is a presence in our lives, something that calls to us from the very edges of our awareness. Something that has been lost, or never yet found. Or perhaps something of both.

2

The Wisdom of
the Dance

If I am aware, each moment is an experience of membership. Unaware, I might not notice the hawk, now circling low outside my window. But if I let it arc into my awareness, the hawk and I are suspended together in a fleeting, fragile moment. When it dives and disappears, I turn to the north. A flock of small birds crests the cypress hedgerow behind the house. The slender green branches at the top nod slightly. The unmown hay below is still.

Membership is offered repeatedly, a tapestry of sunlight and shadow, texture, creatures and earth. In such a moment, I feel *embedded*. I realize I am not merely alone but also integral. In that more resonant state, I am enriched by an abundance of information from the surrounding display. Today, I came down on a foggy morning to find a Monarch butterfly still folded for the night on a screen at the stair landing. I was amazed to see it so close and brought a cup of coffee over to the window. Attracted by the intricate, heavy black web laced on each wing, I pulled up a chair and reached for my drawing pad and colored pens.

The creature was utterly motionless. Only as I finished the drawing, did I see an almost imperceptible flutter of its wings. Then it rubbed its face with one feeler like a sleepy child. I went to refill my cup and when I returned, it was gone.

I went back upstairs to the window seat where I had been reading the night before. Outside, caught in the screen, was another web. A cobweb, thickened with dust and laden with dew, sparkled like diamonds in the early morning light. A single thistle-down fluttered at its center. I opened my book and turned the page. The author began to compare the web of interconnections between neurons with the Buddhist sutra of a network of jewels.

To me, moments in which I experience these kinds of simultaneity—the webs of a butterfly's wing and a spider, webs on a printed page—are extraordinary. Yet I have come to view that very simultaneity as an expression of the ordinary: that which is. The simultaneity extends to my sleep. Last night a dream called me to take my place amidst many rows of people in order to sing in a chorus. It seemed yet another way of reminding myself that I was a small part of a very large community of life.

The question is: how does one learn to sing as a member of the chorus, live as part of the web? How are we to become aware of our embeddedness* and learn to function as an integral part of the whole? These questions have captured my imagination. I believe they are *the questions* of our time.

* Because Integrity refers to a state of being, I have created a few qualitative words such as *embeddedness, boundedness, attunement*. Other important concepts such as a different usage of *embodied* will not be footnoted.

Late afternoon, I take them with me on a walk. I lean against a split rail fence and watch a thousand starlings wheel like a single kite in a frisky wind. Diving, they barely graze the field with their right flank, then lift again in a spiral against an evening sky. A whole flock soars at an angle as precisely as a ballet troop, hangs suspended for a moment, then glides away in reverse. It seems as simple an act as breathing, and as effortless. Turning, soaring, diving, each pattern dissolves into another like the designs of a kaleidoscope turned by the slightest rotation of a wrist.

Sweeping across the transparent sky, this silhouette of the-many-moving-as-one has been deeply imprinted on my imagination since childhood. So have the questions: How do they move as they do? What holds them in the pattern? Is there a signal? A leader?

The New York Times reports recent research on flocking behavior that claims starlings and many other species do not follow a leader; rather, the studies show that each bird operates independently, following some kind of inner guidance for self-protection. What amazes the scientists is that the phenomenon of the flock apparently issues from countless individual decisions—yet its collective wisdom far surpasses the intelligence of individual birds.[1]

Each bird embodies an ancient set of experiences and instructions. At the same time, each is embedded in the life and movement of the flock. What captivates me is the resonance between these two states. *What is good for the individual bird becomes, collectively, a higher intelligence.* There is neither control from a leader nor a signal. It is the wisdom of the dance.

In our cultural lineage we have not danced for a long time. It is hard for us to think in those terms. For centuries our focus has been on the individual—on our separateness—and on the boundedness of objects. It is a function of the kind of thinking we have evolved. Since the time of the Greeks, the type of progress we have made in Western culture has depended on our growing objectivity. We have learned to separate ourselves from the object, tighten our focus, become adept at analysis. By doing so, we have split up reality into that which can be objectively assessed and that which can't. As a result, information which does not square with logic has been discounted and our perception of reality has suffered. I am coming to see how many opportunities for learning we miss, and how much information is lost in the process. In seeking intelligence we have lost our wisdom.

Our skills in logical problem solving have served us well in many ways. At the same time, they cut us off. Our solutions often tend to result in isolated, unintegrated approaches, ungrounded in the needs of the whole.

Many of us often experience ourselves as isolated and unintegrated in the scheme of things as well. Given the tendency to split things apart, we have learned to see in an either-or way. As a result, there exists a powerful tension between being an autonomous individual and being a part of a relationship or group. Moreover, having developed these skills of dissection, we have no *social* means of redeeming or synthesizing what we have taken apart. No wonder the human difficulties within and between groups exist!

Having worked most of my adult life as an organizational consultant, I can't help but reflect that this theme is played out every day in communities and organizations throughout the world. Is it any wonder that organizations find it so difficult to focus on the overall goal and still pay attention to the needs of individuals? On the other side of the fence, individuals may work hard to increase their job skills, but how difficult it can be to work independently and still function as an integral part of a group: to communicate face to face, to deal with conflicts, to make joint decisions and to operate in harmony with a larger plan.

Organizations compound the dilemma by relying on external controls such as formal structures, role definitions, policies or reward systems to maintain group cohesion. More often than not, individuals, grown accustomed to similar external control devices in families, schools and religious institutions, collude with the organization by remaining dependent on it.

I often think of the birds dancing together across the sky and wonder if there is any hope for organizations such as these. If members depend for belonging on *external* definitions of identity, or on direction from a leader, however benevolent, how does that group make any lasting change?

Could we, instead, sustain new ways of group life with *internal*, *individual* change, so that we all might function from a deeper sense of autonomy and responsibility? Might we then start moving toward a new form of cohesion? Something different from control? Something like flocking? *What is good for the individual bird becomes, collectively, a higher intelligence.* Might there be hope of a higher order of functioning by the human group? This possibility would be a very different phenomenon from mob psychology in which individuals *devolve* to a *lower* form of behavior. It implies, rather, a radical *improvement*.

There are precedents for such a phenomenon following a pattern widely seen in nature. There is a principle of *completing* seen in organisms throughout evolution: a resolution at higher and higher levels of complexity, rather than dissolution. "...(T)he *salient characteristic of the evolutionary process...is the **knitting***

29

together of ever-larger wholes of ever-increasing harmony."[2] Thus, over time, we find single-celled creatures banding together to function as a whole sponge; groups of cells specializing to become organs such as stomachs or hearts; and groups of organs functioning collectively as an organism. This is the very essence of *Integrity*.

Integrity takes us past the interpersonal or intrapsychic focus of sociology or psychology because our problems are no longer merely local or personal. At the end of the twentieth century, the social structures on which we have based our sense of individual and group identity are collapsing. Sexuality. Marriage. Family. Community. The economy. Religion. Agriculture. Education. Nation. Other issues are even more enormous. The environment. The disappearance of species. Global suffering.

Thomas Berry asserts that our global problems are so severe, we need to recreate the human at a species level. He states categorically that we need to learn to *function as a species*.[3] What does that mean? How indeed do we begin to face the reality that it is no longer workable to function as billions of separate egos collected in competing nationalities and cultures? How can we learn to experience ourselves as a species?

Because of our tendency to think in an either-or way, most of us, at this point, see ourselves paradoxically, as both too large and too small. As individuals, we loom too large in our own eyes when caught up in our local, separate lives. Thus focused, we lose sight of the complex creation around us. Conversely, when we turn our attention toward our surroundings, we see ourselves too small, and fail to recognize all that is within us, if we but look.

To integrate the one with the many, we will need to change two perceptions: context and identity. First, I believe that a larger sense of group life cannot take hold in old contexts and that a new context, common to all, is needed. All over the world children have listened to stories from their elders about who they are: where they have come from, where they are going and what they are about. I learned about pilgrims and George Washington's cherry tree and wagon trains rolling across the western plains; about slaves coming out of Egypt and a birth in Bethlehem and the golden city of God. Others heard about a Bo tree or a tree at the center of the earth; about Mecca and chariots riding across the heavens; about knights or goddesses or men on walkabouts.

In the context of these stories, we learned how our ancestors arrived at fundamental principles, at guidelines for their lives. We learned what was of value and what was sacred. We learned what made our group unique or how a man or woman should make choices in certain human contexts. But now we have to ask ourselves: how can these stories inform our choices about rainforests and resources, overpopulation and abortion, indigenous nations and political boundaries, progress and pollution?

How can my learnings about democracy teach me what to do in a choice between jobs for humans and the destruction of another species? What do my Judeo-Christian ethics tell me about topsoil flowing into the sea or genetic engineering or a right to die? Can any myth or folk tale from one culture inform a *species* which includes aboriginals and admirals, Native Americans and entrepreneurs?

We need to enlarge our view of what is local. What is our homeland? Who are our people? To what do we belong? To answer those questions, we need to find a way to let the sacred and secular stories at the heart of our cultures rest in a larger context. Our cultural definitions and the rich stories which sustain them are

31

irreplaceable. They need not be lost, but they are too small to address our global needs.

We as a species don't know our story. We are *between stories*. But if we can break through the boundaries of the old ones, we shall come face to face with the vast story of the universe, and feel the awe and wonder of its unfolding. That is the first essential step to a species orientation.

We need to redefine what it means to be human. Integrity is a response to that statement. I learned who I was through relationship: as a daughter to my parents, a sister, a friend on the playground, a member of a team, a graduate of a school, a resident of several New England states. Later I learned who I was as a lover, a musician, a teacher, a mother, a responsible member of our community. My religion taught me that we human beings had dominion over all the animals; my schooling added a breadth of relationship to the wisdom and creativity of many cultures.

But who am I in relation to stars? To glaciers and galaxies, to rainforests in Borneo? What is my relationship to the living and non-living components of our planet? To the entire community of beings?

Integrity radically changes our orientation. It extends our identity inward more deeply than psychology and outward beyond ordinary social and geographic groupings. It is a way of living at depth in ourselves *and* within the context of the earth's journey. It has to do with learning to fly with the flock; a *way of being in the universe*. Then we can experience ourselves as embedded.

Embeddedness is a dimension of Integrity in which there is no longer a dichotomy between the one and the many, but a resonance. Embedded, one has one's own intelligence and identity *and something more*. One is a functioning part of something larger, like cells within a larger organism. Embedded, more dimensions of oneself, others and a larger reality are brought into relationship. The nature of that relationship is different from mere interaction. There develops a reciprocity that goes beyond give and take—it has a quality of being interwoven, given over. There is an increasing intimacy, a permeability of boundaries, even while acknowledging and respecting boundaries.

Our new integrity may resemble a fetus embedded in the womb, possessing its own circulatory system, yet receiving nutrients from the mother's blood to nourish it. Mother and child are attuned to one another, subtly affecting one another.

There are quiet and exquisitely subtle moments in sexual intercourse, when partners are utterly resonant, no longer trying to effect anything for self or other, beyond knowing whether one or the other is the experiencer. At such times our awareness of separateness fades and two beings become one, held momentarily by a sacred bond.

Can we learn this kind of resonance with our species and the earth community? I don't believe that it is something we can *think* our way through. Nor do I believe that we ourselves can make it happen. If, like the flocking birds, the greater competence comes out of the larger organism, not the individuals, all we can really do is make ourselves ready. It will require a willingness to be receptive and to receive the unknown. The event—and it will be an event as cosmically significant as the earth's invention of chlorophyll—is not within our control.

When the chlorophyll molecule was created, it was a *wholly new food from a whole new source* for the organisms on earth. Prior to that, those organisms, the autotrophs, had feasted on the "soup," the substance of their environment, to such a degree that they had eaten it all up. About to starve, they learned to feast on light.[4]

The key to 'making ourselves ready' has to do with finding a *wholly new way of being, one oriented to a whole new source*. We too may have to turn to something less obvious, less logical and seemingly less substantial than anything we've previously known.

By developing a refined receptivity, we may retrieve some of the long lost wisdom of the dance buried deep in our genetic structure. Most of us in Western culture have a dulled receptivity to those strains that used to help human beings stay in step with the great dance of life. We have forgotten how to hear many of the other subtle languages of the cosmos available to us, within and without. We will need to find ways to weave all of these into relationship with the knowledge we have now, for we are choosing not to regress, but to integrate. That is an important choice, for there are also new steps to be learned. *Wholly new ways…*

At the end of the twentieth century, we are searching for wisdom—as individuals and as a species—during a period of tumultuous change on earth. We need to look for some of this guidance within—for much of what we seek is in our *human nature*. Nature is not focused and goal oriented as we were in our organizational efforts. She moves spontaneously like the starlings. As in the dance, some of her steps are backward and some are forward. There is a reciprocity between the not yet and that which has been. She often goes in one direction, in order to reach another. Like the hawk, nature circles and improvises and plays as she works. She is not merely beautiful and creative. She has a dark and destructive side which is profoundly necessary.

If we are to find the way to a fuller humanity, we will discover ourselves in a continual process of letting go of control. We also need to let go of the hope for a leader to rescue us, take risks for us or tell us what to do. Instead, we will need to rely on a different authority—a deep authoritativeness far from our conscious control. Relying as individuals on that authoritativeness beyond our own egos, we may find that we move synchronously too. Not unlike the birds.

In our human nature, it will be our inner lives which will ground us in the life of the whole. Like the birds, it is an attunement to something within each of us which is most needed for our direction. For we are talking about depth. And often it is something quite opposite to what we are intending that calls us to take our first step on the new way.

Part Two

~

A Letting Go

3

The Briefcase in the Garden

Desperately in need of help, I had made an appointment for my lunch hour. Stuffing a sheaf of papers into my briefcase in case I had to wait, I hesitated and swallowed hard behind the door of my small office. Then I stepped out into my department's central reception room, a maze of desks awash in the glare of fluorescent light. The company where I worked had doubled in size to 1500 people in the last year and still had not caught up to the workload. The Xerox machine whined as I surveyed the large room: typewriters clattering as countless phones jangled unanswered, each overworked clerk trying to out-wait the others. "Will somebody please answer the phone!" I cried, knowing it was unprofessional, but feeling at the end of my tether.

I glanced hastily at my appointment calendar, scratched full of abrupt management changes in plan. It was typical of the hyped-up, fast-growth electronics environment of the seventies, but I was reeling from the chaotic and conflicting demands. Our top management group was staffed with brilliant, driven men, engineers who worked days, nights and weekends. They were proud of their "QRC"—"quick response capability"—and wanted results "yesterday" for their unnamed defense department clients.

I was holding on by a frayed thread as I left the office. The freeway was choked with noonday traffic and my body tensed in response. Still, as I drove, I composed a report to my company president. I would complete it at home that evening. I stopped at my house on the way, left a note for the children's sitter, grabbed the mail and wolfed down a banana for lunch as I drove the rest of the way to my appointment, reading the mail at red lights, heart racing.

I found the entrance to the clinic, pushed open the heavy door and found myself unexpectedly in a green cloister. Surrounding it were two stories of windows, some curtained, others not. Overhead the blue sky lighted the garden below. It was spring, and a profusion of blooms bulged from branches all around me: rhododendrons of every color, azaleas, hyacinths, red, purple, pink, white.

The door closed slowly behind me, sealing off the space. What a contrast to the frantic scene I had left at the company. Here in the garden it was utterly quiet. I was early. There was a wooden bench in a corner, and I sat down, leaning up against the warmth of the building behind me, my body wound tight. I had not sat still in a long time. I realized I was still holding my breath and my hand was frozen around the handle of my briefcase. I let it go, and at the same time let my heavy shoulder bag slide off my shoulder. I looked around, amazed that such a serene environment existed in my world.

All around the perimeter of the cloister, under the heavy branches of the shrubs in bloom, someone had carefully raked white sand as in a Japanese garden. Here and there were large round flat stones arranged in random patterns on the sand. Instinctively, I took off my high heeled shoes. With hardly a glance at the windows surrounding me, I walked in my stocking feet over to a sandy bower in the shade. Stepping onto the cool white sand I sat down in the middle of the garden. Then, very slowly, I stretched out full length on the earth. I lay there under the bushes in full view of everyone—in a business suit complete with security badge on the lapel. On the bench in the corner, my purse, shoes and briefcase stood civilized guard.

It was a long time since I had lain on the earth. I didn't understand it then. Mind overwhelmed, my body had simply led me to it. It was a symbolic act: I didn't know I had lost my way. People walked by on the sidewalk, murmuring in pairs as I sifted sand through my fingers, remembering sand; as I looked up through half open eyes at the tenderness of rhododendron blooms close to my face, remembering beauty. As I smelled the hyacinth, remembering the fragrance of flowers.

～

Subsequently, I had a dream:

> I was driving up a mountain road, intent on getting to
> the light at the top. Gradually the way became steep and
> dark and I realized the pavement had ended some time
> back. I was half way up the mountain when the road
> became a series of sharp switchbacks, and no matter
> how hard I pressed on the accelerator, I made no
> progress upward. In desperation I tried all the pedals,

twisted the wheel sharply left and right. As I willed the
car to the top, it halted abruptly.

Then I saw the sign. There, at the right side of the road
was an arrow. The sign said "ONE WAY" and the
arrow pointed back down the way I had come. There
was no doubt about its message:

The way up was down.

As I attempted to become receptive to the subtle language of
my inner story teller, I was amazed. How clearly she taught me! In
her elegance and economy of expression, I saw represented the
striving and exertion and anxiety that had characterized my entire
life; and in the single image of the sign, a teaching:

Stop struggling up the mountain. You cannot reach what you
are really seeking this way. Turn around. Go back down. Start here
where it is dark. The Way is one way, *down*.

The dreamer's advice was not congruent with anything I had
learned in my family or in my education. Nor did it square with
the kind of things I might hear from any of the people surrounding
me. But was it telling me something totally foreign to my nature?
Now I realize that it was only foreign to my *culture* and my own
customary interpretation of reality. More likely, the dreamer comes
out of my real human *nature* and expresses what is best for it. At
the time, however, I had long since left nature: the earth, play, my
body and its wisdom, all were left behind in my childhood. Like a
plant in the straight, homogeneous rows of a garden, I had become
a product of my culture in the fifties: *cultivated*, a "lady." I had
excelled in school and on that foundation of intellectual achieve-

ment I had defined my reality. For decades, I had relied heavily on my wits and my will power.

At mid-life, I was in the midst of a fast-paced and stressful career. Structured for success, I had reached a peak of attainment and at the same time was consumed with fear. With sheer determination, I was trying to meet all the demands of home and work—and I had developed no inner resources for coping with the realities of life.

The dream proposed a mode of being in direct opposition to my own: It offered descent—I had sought always to move upward; it offered a quest—I had been searching for answers; it asked me to enter the unknown—I had spent a lifetime carving security out of what I knew and what I could control.

I experienced the dream as a call to turn around—not just my car—but my hard-driving life. As I contemplated following its instructions, I knew I would be heading into unknown territory—into the dark—and I was terrified.

Perhaps the call to life is sounded repeatedly. While there are many kinds of calls, the message for me was that of Rilke's poem: *"You must change your life!"*[1] The dream did not specify how I was to change my life. It offered a *way*—the same way the adventure on the motorcycle began—in *descent*. Here I despair of language, for this image of the journey down the mountain, as I discovered, had many meanings. In some cases it meant "back" into the past. In others it meant a descent into the body. It implied humility and *creatureliness*. It signified depth.

Much of the rich meaning of the dream, however, had nothing to do with place or finite direction: the journey instead was more toward a state, a *bearing — in every sense of the word.* Toward *Integrity.*

I believe we discover our bearings as we learn to bear the reality of our depths, and more importantly, that those depths we bear reflect the depths of the universe itself. The experience of integrity is the embodiment of those depths. The invitation to journey down is a journey without direction in order to find direction. The place we turn is within, and it is within that we find the tender connection between the one and the many. It is in that tender connection that we find our bearings to function as an integral part of the whole, to fly as members of the human flock.

The call for me was an invitation to the wisdom of the dance, a call into a fuller experience of my humanity. It was a call into a new relatedness: with my body, with others, with the earth community, with the universe. In some mysterious way, by entering deeply into the soft flesh and blood that I am, a way opens into life itself; the membrane permitting communion with members of my species and all of creation is rendered permeable.

I experience this relatedness as more than an intuitive flash or a mystical apprehension. I realize that we are given little clues, tiny hints about the connectedness of all of life *all the time.* If they are followed, we eventually discover we are flooded with reality all day long (and all night in our dreams). This is the question: are we determined to continue viewing life through the narrow crack *we* call reality? Or are we willing to dare the ridiculous, the chaotic, the terrifying and the unknown that swirls about us communicating a reality too vast for intellect? If we are willing, we will have to learn *wholly new ways,* ways foreign to our culture, our beliefs and our thinking.

That, I think, is the call, as we struggle together, daring to discover more of what it means to be a human being. To discover what is real. And the first thing we need to challenge is our *knowing*.

4

Daring Not To Know

If I were to choose the simplest image to represent myself—or reality or the universe—I would choose a circle. It expresses an unbroken entity. No line divides one quality from another; nothing marks a beginning or end. Yet a characteristically human practice has been to snip at that unbroken line and lay it out straight—to place a word at either end and call it truth. In that attempt to take hold of life with words, we create a language of opposites. Now, after thousands of years, we tend to behold our abstractions and call them real.

Surely the great gift of language has been to define, to clarify, to name. How joyfully infants seize on words to lift themselves up out of helplessness into greater self-determination! They recognize those distinctions as a means to an end: the very human hope of gaining control over their environment.

Trouble is, we are now so immersed in language that it has become, as Lewis Thomas would say, our *habitat*. Instead of seeing words as tools to help us relate to our surroundings, they have themselves become our ground. We are literally enmeshed in mass media, in the word culture we have created. Our brains are bathed in language. Our minds run on words the way cars run on gasoline. They are both the source and the medium of our thinking. And without language, we have no conscious memory.

As a result, it is very difficult to get outside our mental constructions and see them for what they are: our creations, a mere few threads culled from the whole. Language gives us the illusion of control by providing distinctions. Yet since any definition—any word—requires us to exclude something in order to use it, language too often sacrifices truth for practicality. It fragments.

One April day on the jagged Sonoma coastline, I sat at the edge of a field with my easel and water colors. The uneven tufts of green meadow grasses were punctuated with purple. The wild iris were in bloom and I had come to paint them. For a while, I found myself naming colors or shapes or direction of movement— "violet," "curved," "upward"—as a way of choosing how to proceed with my brush. Later, I sought words for qualities of texture and fragrance that I could not reproduce. There were none. I gave up. I had been painting one blossom for some time when I suddenly realized how limited analysis was. Ultimately, I just sat there with the iris, and discovered it speaking to me in its own language of *presence*. As I softened my eyes and my focus, I received infinitely more from that living center of being than my words could have expressed.

Words can be a prison. One manner of thinking which has most imprisoned me has been the importance of choosing between the poles of language: male—female, black—white, old—young, rich—poor… With the addition of words such as good—bad, right—wrong, we shift from description to judgment and exclusion. By forming opposites with our words, we polarize the culture in which we live, and fragment the world. In such an airtight environment, how can reality ever find a way in?

Once, thirty years ago, a different view of reality erupted so dramatically it still impacts my life. I lay in an operating room. Just before coming out of the anesthesia, a vast image loomed before me. It appeared to be a sphere whirling in one direction, and a sphere whirling in the opposite direction, *except they were both the same sphere*. It was a vivid declaration, and on awakening I announced to the nurses and doctors, "I've just seen the Truth!" "Yeah, yeah, that's what they all say," was the bored reply.

Though the image I received in that less focused mental state is still crystal clear, my every-day mind cannot grasp how a single entity could revolve in two directions at once. This mind— steeped in a culture that deifies logic and then defines itself through a narrow lens of reason—cannot tolerate the mystery of *not knowing*. It begs me instead to decide between opposites—to choose either one or the other.

Recently I have come to think of my brain as a sea anemone, that tender low-tide creature which looks like a many-petalled flower. For much of my life my mind grasped at answers as the anemone clutches tightly around a passing object in the flow. My *perpetual focus* walled everything else out. Now I balance that tension by also imagining my brain an *open* anemone, a still being, petals stretched wide to the flow, letting the ocean swirl through, taking what comes and letting the rest go. A receiver.

Such was the quality of openness I permitted myself on the motorcycle journey. That day, once I let go of schedule and destination, softened my gaze and welcomed all possibilities, the world entered. Since then, it has not been easy to stop confining my world with facts, for the habit is very ingrained. Having answers had long helped me to frame my reality—answers like knowing where things were…what was expected…what would happen. To the degree I had language to define a situation, I thought I "understood" it. I was safe from the chaos of not knowing.

As a result of my experience on the motorcycle trip, I began to look at my childhood training in language, knowledge and control. Surely, when I was a young child, a single word helped me sort out reality: was a four-legged animal a cat or a dog, a horse or a sheep? There was always a correct definition and I was rewarded at home and in school for right answers. Language defined categories of beings and objects. It clarified sets of actions. It named my world. But often language evaluated all these things as well, and therein lay much of its power. For hidden beneath the layers of naming and grouping, much language had moral roots.

As I was being taught what were appropriate behaviors and attitudes for civilized human life, I was subject to responses that discriminated between "good" and "bad" *all the time*. (*"What a bad little girl!…Aren't you ashamed of yourself?…That's not good for you…What a good dog!…Good girls don't do that…It's bad to do that…"*) Those words are deeply carved in my memory. Only recently have I understood the powerful links between that early morality and my survival instincts. For surely there is a part of every one of us, even as very young children, which recognizes our dependence on our parents. And surely there is a part which believes that if we do things to displease them, our very lives are at risk.

I remember a wish I made repeatedly from the time I was about four years old:

I was in my bed. I had been spanked because I had done something bad, but I didn't know what it was. Worse, I didn't know what good was. I curled myself into a tight ball under the scratchy blue blanket and tried to figure it out so it wouldn't happen again. As I cried into my soggy feather pillow, I wished for a beautiful fairy to give me a ring that would pinch me when I was bad, so I would know. And then I promised myself with a litany that had carried me into sleep for as far back in my short history as I could remember: "But tomorrow... Tomorrow I'm going to be good!"

My confusion lay in the fact that I could no longer rely on what was inside my own being to inform me of what was "the right way to be." The basis for that judgment was something quite arbitrary *and* outside of me: things which felt quite natural and desirable to me were often punishable; and things which were quite unpleasant and unnatural to me were praised and rewarded. So I learned to become quite vigilant, watching others for clues to guide me and letting that kind of decision—good/bad, right/wrong, true/false—undergird much of my thinking. Conscious or unconscious, the requirement to evaluate, often between morally loaded opposites, framed my world view. How I felt about myself, how I conceived of authority, the friendliness of the universe, all were colored by this dimension of judgment.

This survival-based morality is rooted even more deeply in us, however; even more than a learned response, it is biological. Some of the earliest life forms foraging for nourishment needed to define what was "me" and what was "not me" in order not to consume themselves! These early biological decisions were the basis for their survival. Today, those same decisions are the basis for ours:

Our immune systems protect us from infection and disease. In order to do that, they must have a way to distinguish between "me" or "not me." Only then can they set out to destroy foreign organisms or potentially destructive tissue within our bodies.

We can trace this early life decision through the branching pathways of evolution: from a cell knowing its boundaries, to a creature of prey knowing its predator, through to the socialization practices of mammals. If one imagines a mother bear cuffing her cub in displeasure, it is still clear that even these kinds of judgments are rooted in *biological* morality. They sustain survival.

Yet something changes when we come to the so-called ultimately "moral animal" created by civilizations. Here, the full weight of a mechanism of choice rooted in biology turns abstract. An intellectual world-view of opposites carved out of language, and often loaded with judgment, displaces nature's wisdom evolved over millennia, and calls itself reality. Then, the inner conversation of each child as it searches for an identity might sound something like this:

> *Me or not me: I am good. I am not bad. I have these qualities. I do not have those qualities. This is what it means to be a worthy person. That is not a worthy person. A female is...A male is not...Blacks are...Mexicans are not...Democracy is...Socialism is not...This is true...that is false...*

This is an example of the dualistic basis for "knowing." Such thinking requires choices between one pole or another. There is a necessity to *decide*, a word from the same root as *matricide* and *fratricide*, meaning *"to kill a part of."* In order to live in a world of duality, *something must be negated.* It is as if we are asking our brains to operate only in a binary system, like the yes/no states of a computer.

What does that kind of polarization do to our beings? To our very sense of self and of life? We often rely on the artist to express intuitive connections of this sort. In a work entitled *"The Friendly Gray Computer,"* the painter, Keinholtz, depicts a shiny steel computer about five feet tall, plugged into the wall, large dials behind it glowing. On closer look, one sees two chubby toddler legs protruding from the front, as if the flesh and blood of a child had been fed into it. That image of a toddler eaten alive is so powerful one almost doesn't notice that the computer has the base of a rocking chair. Keinholtz has created a vivid portrayal of what duality does to us even as we learn language in our parents' laps.

~

As I was beginning to heed the call to change my life, almost all of my assumptions and definitions were being challenged. Cast in ideas—in language—they represented what I *knew*. My identity. My beliefs. My mental habitat. Yet I had begun to recognize that *images* such as the iris, the sphere whirling in two directions, the sea anemone, and the *Friendly Gray Computer* hinted at a richer and more complete reality than words could express.

Images are a deeper way of knowing, a means of communication *prior* to language. Before we could speak, we saw. In evolution, our ability to *imagine* preceded language. "What does an animal recognize when it comes upon another animal?...Its text is the living form."[1] Images are a language of the cosmos more complex than words; they speak directly to our bodies. They reach into our souls.

Beginning to trust my images was the next step on the downward way. Little did I realize that I was embarking on a sacred journey; one that would lead me to a new, more authentic identity and a clear sense of belonging to the universe.

The single vivid image in the following dream let me know in no uncertain terms the trap I was in and the terror I felt at the prospect of letting go of my world view. At the same time, the picture held a promise, and its power propelled me to risk what felt like my life:

> *I was slung between two enormous concrete buttresses,*
> *sagging like a hammock and holding on for dear life.*
> *Belly down, my hands clawed at one pier and the tops*
> *of my feet dug at the other. Peering beneath me, I saw a*
> *river flowing far below, between the two massive*
> *parapets. I was terrified that I would lose my grip and*
> *plunge into the water.*

There in the dream was a concise image of my world: hung between poles literally cast in concrete, I was a captive of what I knew. Reality, as a flowing river, moved beneath me. But in my efforts to be "safe," I had driven that rich dimension of life far from awareness. Clinging to the rigidities of definition and certainty, I could not receive the living world through the abstractions I had constructed. In fact, the parapets symbolized the waking dream and they isolated me from the wonder and vitality of being truly awake. Alive. Instead I was separated. Bounded. My thinking had created an artificial world of limits, roles and judgments. I was a successful product of my culture, and no longer lived in the world of flesh, blood and living tissue that I was. Instead, I lived an illusion—the illusion of knowing.

I could not avoid the implications of the dream in the days that followed. It challenged the framework I had relied on for a lifetime. I knew I needed to exercise choice and make evaluations. I knew I needed boundaries. But the dream was emphatic: I also needed to lose them at times. Somehow, I needed alternative ways of being in the world and I had no way to imagine them. At that very moment in my life, I saw the *yin-yang* symbol for the first time and realized it was like a two-dimensional version of the sphere I had envisioned coming out of anesthesia. It was not a neat, black and white mandala of polarities, nor was it static like the concrete towers of my dream. Instead, it represented the polar forces of the world in constant motion: turbulent, black tumbling into white, white into black, yet each transforming into the other, each having the other at its heart. That new image offered me hope.

Gradually, the practise of attending to images began to evolve my thinking. I realized that whether I was thinking about knowledge, personhood or community, *all* was needed for the whole. It became clear that I would not heal without including—indeed embracing—differences and all varieties, in others and in myself. It also became clear that reality was replete with the same variety.

The oversimplified circle would not suffice to symbolize the diversity I'd begun to see. Neither would the *yin-yang* symbol, however dynamic. Eventually, an image came to mind of a rubber ball I'd had as a child. It was translucent and marbled throughout: a multitude of brilliant colors like swirling and tangled threads. In the ball, the action of the swirls was stopped. But if reality were something like that ball before it hardened—huge as the universe and still being stirred in the cauldron of ongoing creation— imagine the changing textures of experience, the continuous coming together and parting of different colored "events;" the confusion of color, no-color, mixtures and movement, past and future. And bubbles of nothing as well. What a symbol of chaos!

The terror I felt at the message of the dream was, in part, a terror at this kind of chaos and confusion. But the dream, reflecting the conditions of my life at the time, showed me that I had hardened just like the ball. Its message was literally a call to let go: it dared me *not to know*. If I were to change my life as Rilke proclaimed, my *thinking* would have to be the first thing to change. If I responded, I knew I would not be able to hold on to my definitions and right answers. I quaked before such an unknown with no idea of its form or content.

Little did I know of the untold gifts that awaited me. Gifts in myself. Gifts in the universe. Nor could I imagine the richness around me that I was soon to discover, richness that was a direct result of chaos. For in the strange new world I was about to enter, confusion was not only all right but something to be prized.

Weary of perpetual focus, I began to open my mind to the possibility that images might contain some wisdom along with my intellect. Something in me, however frightened, also hoped. Perhaps it believed I was being summoned to something real.

And so I imagined myself a caterpillar at the very tip of a branch with no place else to go. With great effort I gathered all that I really trusted under me like my rear legs. And then, very slowly, I stretched my head forward, groping, out into the dark.

5

Entering the Dark

I was alone. Afraid of the dark. I felt like I did when I was a child, because I *didn't know*. I was starting over, learning how to learn, and no one was there at the end of the branch to teach me. All I could do was try to be patient and wait for the unknown.

As time went by, I began to feel the first of many strange sensations in my body. It felt as if someone had both hands around my throat, strangling me. The sensation plagued me for two years. Longing for relief, I tried every approach I knew: physical, emotional, intellectual. The strangling was relentless. Sometimes I felt helpless. Yet I discovered that I had to learn to welcome and honor that helplessness, for in those moments when I gave up, pieces of truth gradually emerged. The teacher which had come forth to guide me through a labyrinth of learning for several years was my own body, and I only seemed to understand its message after I had tried everything else I knew—and failed.

In that state, one day, I mindlessly cradled my neck between my fingertips. All of a sudden entirely new thoughts erupted in me: *My neck. It's the connection between my head and my body. A dark passageway. A descent.*

New questions flooded my awareness. *Whose hands are around my throat? Who doesn't want communication between my body and my head?* As the new answers emerged, they startled me: *It's me! I am the strangling one! I'm the one who doesn't want to know what's hidden there.*

I realized with some embarrassment that while I was groping into the dark, I was at the same time fighting against it every inch of the way. *So. I am a house divided.*

Who I was—my "I"—was my intellect. Until that moment, if I gestured to myself, I pointed to my head. Once I recognized that I was a mind cut off from my body, I started to build a bridge between this unknown being below my neck and "me." First, I became aware that the strangling feelings were triggered by my own thoughts. Sometimes my throat felt squeezed as I interacted with people, other times when I read the newspaper or a book. One thing was becoming clear: on this journey down into my body, the old way I had solved problems wasn't going to work. I was not able to reduce my discomfort by trying to analyze or "figure it out." I had to learn to wait until something new and creative emerged of its own accord.

In the meantime, I was clearly afraid of this unknown. When I'd imagined myself the caterpillar, I had gathered all that I trusted under me like my rear legs. Now it was apparent that if I was to continue probing the confusion, I would have to rely on them for my stability. Some of that trust was in people. I was blessed, in particular, by the presence of two women who guided and sustained me. I also relied heavily on a set of spiritual disciplines. In addition, I did not abandon my intellect. And I was immensely encouraged by the confirmation I found in the writings and experiences of others. One writer who repeatedly encouraged me was Fritz Kunkel:

> *If the desire to be honest is greater than the desire to be "good" or "bad," then the terrific power of one's vices will become clear. And behind the vice, the old forgotten fear will come up (the fear of being excluded from life) and behind the fear the pain (the pain of not being loved) and behind this pain of loneliness the deepest and most profound and most hidden of all human desires: the desire to love and to give oneself in love and to be a part of the living stream we call brotherhood. And the moment love is discovered behind hatred, all hatred disappears.*[1]

I trusted those words. They held out a promise I fervently wanted to believe. Greater than the force of my fear was the force of a yearning I'd felt for a lifetime. More than anything else, I wanted to love. And I realized I had no idea what that meant.

When the going got rough, I read and re-read the passage. Its wisdom proved true. The price for relief from physical pain and discomfort was a kind of honesty that became a guiding force in my life—an honesty with myself about who I really was. About my beliefs. My feelings. My actual goodness. And badness. If I was to have relief from the strangling, I would have to let go the concrete barricades of my dream, and enter the living stream. I would have to be a receiver, open to whatever was pushing up from my body and *learn to receive myself.*

Until now, I had depended for direction on a disembodied intellect. Without access to tangible, earthy reality, *knowing* had blocked my ability to receive the subtler signals of my body. Gradually I became willing—always under the duress of physical pain—to know what my body knew. As I became more determined to trust these strange promptings regardless of what I found, I took the first steps toward becoming the wide "dish" I had imagined on the motorcycle. I began to understand that the strangling occurred in situations when I was angry and afraid to admit it. Or feeling anxiety. Or anguish.

I have known many people who have opted for surgery to relieve the kinds of pain I describe in the pages that follow. One man permanently forfeited the use of his right arm to have a nerve severed. Others have had vertebrae fused, while still others have turned to medication. There are many paths and many solutions. Given my particular bodymind, I would have deprived myself of a rich source of growth and discovery—as well as permanent relief— had I not decided to trust the several sources of wisdom which, together, led me in a new direction.

I am not suggesting that my path is for everyone. In part, my story may confirm others' experience. More important, I hope to encourage the choice *to develop a creative relationship to one's own life and own set of circumstances.* Too often, it seems, we codify one person's creativity into a religion or a science and treat it as if it's an answer. My intent here is rather to encourage the *enlivening experience of one's own creativity*, and the incredible satisfaction and healing that *may* come from it.*

---

* My own experience has been confirmed recently by the teachings of Richard Moss, M.D. who gives many examples of individual creative responses to illness and subsequent healing in his conferences. Most recent of his writings is *How Shall I live? Where Spiritual Healing and Conventional Medicine Meet* (Berkeley: Celestial Arts), 1985.

I had gathered many legs under me, among them a growing trust in intuition and in the roots of language. In an intuitive flash one day I realized that my neck was much like a snake. Its shape, its bony structure and the way it functioned as a passage were like a vestige from the past, an evolutionary legacy. My imagination caught fire. In the ancient myth of the Garden, it was the snake which offered the first opportunity to *decide*—the fruit of the tree of knowledge of good and evil. Right and wrong. Good and bad. I ran to the dictionary and sought the roots of language. Anger came from the Latin *angere*, meaning to choke, strangle or squeeze. With mounting excitement I looked up *anguish* and *anxiety:* the basis for all three words was *angere*. And *its* root was *anx*, meaning *snake!* Had I, once upon a time, *decided* and *killed a part of myself?* Was my inability to let my body speak the result of an early attempt to be good? Might that early myth of the snake (also a symbol of healing in other cultures), be a timeless way of speaking the truth of our bodies to the countless generations of western culture? If so, if I could receive its meaning, then it might literally heal my pain.

I searched the dictionary further: The root of *angina* (for heart disease) was the same. My family was rife with the disease. My father had died from a heart attack only a few years before.

I was startled by the next entry in the dictionary. The "obsolete" meaning of anger was *the smart or pain from a wound*. I remembered reading about the raging response to life of the griefstruck wounded child* and wept. These simultaneous intuitions and events provided the encouragement I needed to go forward; to begin to open my heart to a child long hidden within.

*The wounded child, a term coined by Alice Miller, is the infant who loses his or her own self in an attempt to accommodate the needs of a parent who was similarly wounded. Children such as these become mirrors for their parents' needs and feelings and become alienated from their own. See Miller's *Prisoners of Childhood* (New York: Basic Books, 1981), since republished under the title *The Drama of the Gifted Child.*

As I felt and accepted the snake—the anger, anxiety and anguish—long buried in my body, the phantom hands at my throat let go. The snake had been like the tarantula and the bull on the motorcycle journey, all of them mythical dark keepers of the gate to the downward way. Now the gateway was open.

But I had just begun. No sooner had my throat released than I sensed something new rising within me. Some deeper promptings which I couldn't identify began coming up from inside my abdomen and chest over a long period of time. I felt them as *impressions*, and the form they took, quite unexpectedly, was poetry.

The poem which follows began with a palpably vulnerable sensation in my midsection. I knew I wanted to give the sensation expression but had no idea how. I didn't feel the usual preludes to emotion: tears or tension or heightened energy. Nor was there a familiar word that came to mind. So I sat hunkered down before the keyboard of my word processor and waited, eyes closed. After a while I saw a rose in my mind's eye. Feeling very uncertain, I wrote a line. Then my eye travelled down its long stalk. I wrote two more. Though much of my life I'd wanted to appear tall and firm like a stalk, what had motivated me to write that day was a new, much less solid feeling at depth. What was it? Then the image suddenly hit me. I cried in recognition and wrote the last lines.

❧

IN THE DARK

Far beneath
the petals
unfolding
round a heart—

Far down the upright stalk
bearing the bloom

Farther still,
embedded deep in the moist earth
the root
nurses at the ground.
Tender.
No wonder it is hidden
in the dark.

~

Tenderness was a gift, a quality I had always wanted. No wonder I hadn't known what the sensation was: this was the first time I remembered experiencing it as my own. It was a gift of the dark.

In this mysterious way, poetry became my "golden string."* It became a way to begin to express a me who had been hidden for a lifetime—a me quite without judgments as to "good" or "bad". A me who was real. The poetry was not constructed. It was *received*.

It was an event. I was finding my own voice. And as I found it, sensation and image and feeling and thought became one, traced a path through my body and left footprints.

---

* William Blake: *I give you the end of a golden string*
 Only wind it into a ball
 It will lead you in at Heaven's gate
 Built in Jerusalem's wall.

David V. Erdman, Ed., *The Complete Poetry and Prose of William Blake*, Newly Revised Edition (New York: Anchor Books, 1982), p. 231.

FUNDUS

Like a thong
threaded through the top
of a soft leather pouch,
I draw me closed,
linking my losses -
a tight necklace
of unarticulated grief
around a full throat.

I kept writing from March until December and it wasn't until
then that I began to see the previous nine months for what they
were—a gestation period:

TENDER

I feel tremulous,
throat full
(is it tears or a song?)
before the approach of something
unseen and long forgotten.
Advent-tender,
as if I were about to be known.

HESITATION BEFORE BIRTH

If I come forth,
Will you be there?
Will you see who I am?

If I come forth
Will you greet me
Will you call me by name?

If I cry out,
will you hear me

Will you meet me
here, where I am?

❧

I realized after writing this poem, that the person I wanted
there to greet me was myself. But my relationships were changing
too, and the competent consultant with her briefcase began to
show another side to her husband.

❧

UNDERNEATH

I did not want to know
that I was so afraid.
Or needed you so much
(or anyone at all).

It has been too long
that I have wrapped my cloak around me.

I did not know I was
so small inside.

~

I called these truthful gifts from the darkness my *feelings* and differentiated them from *emotion*. I could literally feel them. They were of flesh and blood. They lived deep in my tissue, in my organs and bones. They could never be disembodied like knowledge or emotion.

It became important for me to recognize the complementary relationship between emotions and feelings. As I now use the word, emotion is an outward expression, closer to the idea of "emoting," often with an express purpose of influencing others. Emotions moved out of me. Feelings, on the other hand, often just stayed inside. They taught me about myself and about life. They *in-formed* me. They were the first fruits of the opening on the downward way.

Because we are each different, I expect that the gifts of the dark are different for each of us. Another person might find bravery and physical prowess, still another, humor, or healing from disease. What emerges is the unique creativity of our own being, to which no one else can give us the key. For someone like me, who had patterned myself on a culture that emphasized strength and performance, competitiveness and achievement, the gifts of vulnerability were what I needed to balance my soul. But the gifts go beyond feelings, as we shall see. *Most important, they go beyond the individual*.

These gifts of the dark are, I believe, the key to living as one among many. They teach us about the inner *and* the outer and how they are connected. As I learned about what my body was saying, I was also making my first tentative forays into learning how I was related to the earth.

TO A CHERRY TREE IN BLOOM

I gaze in wonder
at your breathtaking moment.
You speak syllables of a language
known only to my heart.

And:

FIRE[2]

So!
The earth has fire in her belly.
Well, so do I.

As these offerings from the dark are redeemed, they become gifts of aliveness. And through them, we humans have an opportunity to reclaim our relatedness to the rest of a universe that is alive. We discover that we belong, that we are embedded. If we are to experience our embeddedness, however, we must first become *embodied*. To function as an integral part of the whole, we first need to descend into our bodies, begin to *inhabit* them, and so doing, find what we have lost in the dark.

Though the bright stars and planets continue to mark their course across the daylit sky, it is only in the dark that we can turn to them for direction. And though the cosmos continues to speak to us in many languages, we cannot receive any of these messages—and use them to get our bearings—until we darken the sharp focus of our intellect. Like the brilliance of the sun, it obscures the other languages of the cosmos which are available to us. These languages are the real human habitat, and they are as subtle a presence as the starlight compared to the sun. Like the stars, they provide the necessary context we have lost because of our tense, so-called "objective" focus, a context with as great a perspective as the night sky.

We limit our ability to commune with—and thereby creatively respond to—the realities of the rest of creation when we limit our concept of language to those that are taught by the culture (such as words, math, art or architecture). Further, most of these languages consist of *expressions* or *messages sent*. To redress the balance, I would like to suggest that what we most need to learn from now are *impressions*, or *messages received*.

Over the millennia of evolution, nature has encoded much of the wisdom of the universe in our bodies, our psychic and genetic structures. Yet as we have developed the formidable intellect in some parts of the human species, we have severely limited our perceptions of what we know to "brain knowledge," known as cultural coding.* We have lost the ability to receive and discern

---

* Cultural coding is the term Thomas Berry uses referring to the human extension of genetic coding: the experiences and learning of human culture as it is passed on through educational processes over the generations.

the previously encoded "body knowledge." Rather than leaving this wisdom behind on the human journey, I think it is essential that we stop, reclaim and integrate all those other ways of knowing.

For us, these ways require a new beginning; learning new ways to learn. Rather than from experts or books, this kind of learning requires our presence to and patience with the unknown. As with the stars, it is hard to see clearly until we adjust to the dark.

Thomas Berry, in his plea for human wisdom in the ecological age, asserts our need for greater sensitivity to the entire earth community.[3] Brian Swimme declares that "Life is the development of ever greater sensitivity...We are alive with the desire to awaken that sensitivity!"[4] Ah, yes, but don't we hold it at bay with as much energy? We may claim to want it, but do we really want to bear the cost?

What *is* sensitivity anyway? Is it merely an increase of our sensory perception? Do we strain to see more with our eyes that we may see beauty? Is it making the effort to hear others, to understand them better? Is it deepening our taste, our tactile sense, or all our other senses?

For me, there is a problem with the word. It connotes something we can *do*, implies we have the power. It is, perhaps, too easy a word for this culture to hear and then to dismiss. We called it sensitivity training in the sixties and tried to remove our own and others' blinders. We discovered that it wasn't something we could do.

What if we were to name it *tenderness?* *That* is a word which would not be much appreciated in our culture. But my imagination tells me that it is closer to the nub of it, for tenderness is a

69

dimension of presence. We cannot simply *be* with a flower or a tree or another person—nor can we be receptive to life in all of its manifestations—unless we are tender. Tenderness combines vulnerability with an exquisite experience of vitality.

The snake at my throat was trying to protect me. It guarded the gateway not only to my body, but also to the human vulnerability hidden in the dark. But it kept me from knowing what was *true*. Becoming tender, becoming flesh—the real, vulnerable human beings that we are—creates an honest container for the rest of the journey.

Thereafter, to maintain the path requires more: a new way of setting our course, and a new kind of strength that is different from control.

6

The Compass Bearer

The old ways I viewed myself no longer worked. The elements that were "me" were beginning to crumble and I had nothing with which to replace them. Before I undertook this downward journey, I might have described myself as a balloon tied firmly at the neck, my body a dangling string. Located in my head were my identity and beliefs about what was true. "I" was mother, wife, friend, widow, consultant, musician. I was other things as well: intellect, searcher. I was strong. I was in process. I tried to be loving, and believed I lived as best I could according to what I had learned was right.

One afternoon, I sat in my back yard stunned by two newspaper quotations about love. One was by Anne Landers:

> *Love is a friendship that has caught fire. It is quiet understanding, mutual confidence, sharing and forgiving. It is loyalty through good and bad times...It makes allowances for human weaknesses. Love is content with*

the present, it hopes for the future, and it doesn't brood over the past...

The other was from 1st Corinthians 13:

...Love is patient and kind; love is not jealous or boastful; it is not arrogant or rude. Love does not insist on its own way; it is not irritable or resentful...Love bears all things, believes all things, hopes all things, endures all things...

The expressions were different, both wise. As I looked from one to the other, my jaw dropped. It was as if I'd seen them for the first time. Seen myself for the first time. *I don't have the slightest idea how to love.* I was shattered.

Bit by bit, my self image was being challenged. The dreamer had commented on how stuck I was when I found myself slung like a hammock between two concrete pillars. I realized then, that I tried to hold on to definitions of myself and the world by knowing. Now, as I held instead to a desire to be honest, that same knower in me tried to evaluate the new feelings and portions of my identity as fast as they emerged from the dark. I was not alone. Along with my turbulent culture, I struggled with archaic definitions of "good" feelings and "bad" feelings that simply wouldn't stay boxed in; with practices and patterns that could no longer be labelled "masculine" or "feminine"; with trying to make sense out of that which would not be labelled or categorized.

Accustomed to splitting reality into opposites, I did not know how to deal with these polarities when both were present. In an attempt to regain some sense of order, I sought a symbol to contain them. For months I wrestled with the image of Point Lobos on the

California coast, an image which later became my teacher. Trying
to put my thoughts into words, I wrote:

> Lobos, that dynamic intermingling of massive rock
> and turbulent sea: Robinson Jeffers says it's the
> most beautiful meeting place of land and sea in the
> world! The rocks have been etched and sculpted in
> endless variety, yet stand proud sentinels as the
> water swirls, licks and then recedes to gather itself
> for a renewed onslaught. For an eternity the dialog
> has been unceasing: rock and ocean, male and
> female, form and possibility. Both poles are needed
> for life, for creativity, for meaning. In dialog, each is
> shaped by the other. Yet our culture clings to logic,
> sets the other arena apart, divides the land from the
> life-giving water and calls it progress.

But none of my comfortable categories and opposites worked.
As I examined the container I had tried to construct, I realized
that the rocks I had seen as a symbol of stability would not stay
where I had put them! They were not fixed. Instead, they were at
midpoint in a long metamorphosis, from boiling lava to the soil we
depend on. In the same way, the ocean (which I had defined as
chaotic), seemed the essence of stability when I attended to its
rhythmic and continuing presence. I could not split them into
opposites. *Both* were a source of life and both of chaos.

Likewise, as I journeyed into the depths of my own body, a new
reality broke the bonds of language and identity. As I began to feel
and claim increasing sensations and feelings, what I experienced as
me was different. Inhabiting my body at lower and lower levels, I
found myself saying "me" and pointing not to my head, but to my

torso. It was the beginning of an identity which would eventually extend much further.

No longer a string dangling from an inflated balloon, I was becoming embodied. Thus animated, something had to change. Sustaining the awareness and intense aliveness that was growing in me required more strength than control could provide, more wisdom than the social expectations and moral choices my culture offered me. The issue was not that judgment was wrong, but that *judgment was not balanced by anything else*. I was a whole being, more than a mind. And it was not possible to apply culture's dicta below the neck.

If I was going to be a receiver and accept more of my own— and life's—reality, I would need a new way of finding stability and direction. A dream then offered me an alternative to "concrete" polarities:

> *I stand on the coastline at Point Lobos, sighting along the edge of the sea far into the distance. I have decided to take a journey into the wilderness all along that shore. A woman with me notices I have no compass to guide me and hands me hers. It is round and something like a toy I had as a child. Under its dome, there is neither needle, nor marking for north. Instead a small circle has been cut out of the center of the compass card. To find my way, I am to roll it gently back and forth until a tiny, cone-shaped spiral shell* drops into the opening at the center. (See Figure 1.)*

---

* This shell was like the inch-long augur shells I collected on the west coast of Florida. The shell prefigured the more complex image of spiral descent which is elaborated in Figure 2.

Figure 1

Instead of a spiral shell, the toy I'd had as a child had little ball bearings which one rolled around until they settled in small holes. Perhaps the dream was suggesting that what I needed was not a direction or a destination, but to get my *bearings*. As I understood it, I would get my bearings in entirely new ways, not from polarities, but from the center. Maybe I could rest there like the shell and be in balance?

What mystery! I had heard the term "center" for years, but I didn't know what it meant. (Nor do I believe it is definable. On this journey into depth, as the last two dreams have made clear, we have already passed the point where definitions obtain.) I struggled for a long time to locate my center. One spiritual practice locates it mid-brain, between the two hemispheres and imagines it as a room to be furnished. For me, this is an unfortunate location, since the last place I want to look for my center is in my head!

The martial arts tradition locates a bodily center below the navel. Surely being in one's body is closer to the truth than the previous example. But all of this is like the process of trying to "locate God!" (Is God in heaven or in us, transcendent or not, male or female?) Mystery will not squeeze itself into our little categories. It does not belong to space and time.

Instead, my experience of center has been an evolving one. At first, it was the merest suggestion of a different place in myself to reside. Accustomed to being animated with people, extroverted, I had lived more on the periphery of myself, reacting automatically to events and conversations. I felt I was always "on." As I began to be aware of that tendency, I questioned it. Did I need to have a ready answer, to make conversation, to be responsive? If I wanted relief from the life I had lived, might there be an alternative?

Change was exceedingly difficult. I tried turning off my "on button." Without the protection of an immediate response, I felt naked, my tenderness exposed. As I remained quiet in a social situation, I was afraid people would think me stupid. Over time, as I very slowly pulled back from my edges, I realized I could *stop*. Then, I began to delight at the beginnings of a more inward place to *be*. I was relieved by the peacefulness I felt, and appreciated the opportunity to be thoughtful, to reflect. So doing, I found my view of the world—and myself—changing.

RESERVE

From inside
reserve
feels like a baby's solemn stare

undefended
yet not given over
A place from which to see

It became a place from which to live and create: space to dance. And as my college-age son gently suggested one morning at breakfast, it made more room for others, too.

My experience of center then evolved to a *quality*. This was a quality of being receptive to my experience. Having a bearing is different from being on top of things. It is more a settling in, a readiness to look and listen in new ways. *A willing hum. A tuning in.* The signals at first were faint, because I had so much else cluttering up my space. I needed to learn to be quiet. To empty out. It was a time for *unlearning* opinions, practices and very deep beliefs. Gradually, I let go of the weak and lost parts of myself until there came a time when there was no longer anything in me that I could call *me*. As I learned to tolerate and to trust this undefined space, the center began to emerge.

Simultaneously, I became aware of a vast context for my life. While I focused on an immediate activity, I was often aware of my whole environment at the same time. At times that environment was local, at others my awareness extended to the earth itself, to the universe, to the presence of the mystery. In this way, center began to evolve as a *new orientation*. Turning my attention to this orientation, rather than to a destination or goal, was the heart of getting my bearing. I could attend to my most immediate activity and, at the same time, to the radiant surroundings in which I lived.

It was like learning to live in "middle" kinds of spaces, as if I were in a doorway between waking and sleeping, conscious and unconscious, inside and outside—a place where I might learn from both worlds at the same time. Center was still. Empty. Yet filled with the present. Alive.

I came to appreciate the twilight. It was another doorway, a *between time* which was neither day or night. It had its own quality of place and time, of color and definition that was like *a crossing over*. (This is what metaphor provides, and why, I suppose, I lapsed into poetry so much of that year. Metaphor literally *bears meaning across** the polarities of logic and mystery, of language and body. This is yet another dimension of "bearing.") One night, sitting silently in the twilight—*it is so soft a time, so edgeless*—I came as

---

* From the Greek: *metapherein*, to transfer; *pherein*, to carry, *meta-*, beyond.

close to that qualitative experience of center as I know how to express:

～

LIGHT

Quite unexpectedly
as I sat alone at dusk,
I felt the clear sound of the flute
pierce like a laser,
touch a tiny spot within
where I am neither
experiences nor emotions -
a holy, shining space.

～

Somehow, as I oriented myself in that way, I discovered center as a *state*. A way of being open and empty. It was a paradox. When I was most empty with another person (or with the twilight, or nature), I also felt most present. Presence *and* absence became a *whole thing*, more than the sum of the two. This created a tremendous feeling of aliveness in me, almost a sound, like a timbre.

The new compass lent balance to the subtle dance I was learning between myself and my surroundings. Instead of poles, I was offered a center; instead of an individual destination, an orientation to context. As I learned to be present to that which surrounded me, I began to experience the presence of the other in response, as with the wild iris. Much as I had always loved nature, it was as if I had never before been at home in it. Now, I became aware of the *mutual presence* of all life. I not only belonged, I was embedded. Embodied and embedded, I felt a reciprocal relationship between center and surround; between myself as a center and all the centers around me—trees, persons, plants, creatures. Freed from the wearying tension of logic and control, the limitations of my culture, I had gained a new perspective. I felt both smaller and larger: smaller as I recognized the mysteriousness of all of these centers existing in the vastness of which I am a part; larger as I sensed at the same time the value of my own and every being to the whole creation.

These statements alone, for me, become faith—faith, not as a belief but as a *way of life*. It means that *how I do myself matters to the whole*. It also means that I can attune myself to the whole and get my true bearings for my life, *there*. Like the bearings one gets in relation to the many centers of the night sky, this orientation became the stability and balance I needed to supplant my old ways.

The form of the dream compass itself represents the completeness of which we are each a part:

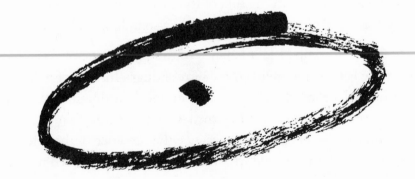

We are enfolded. Center and circumference resonate. In that indescribable dance, they begin to dissolve and transform into one another. But which is the center? Which the circumference? Again I discovered that, in the reality larger than my logic, they could not be split. The center is both center and the encompassment of my identity.

Ultimately, as these boundaries between definitions give way, I experience the center as both container *and* contained.* It becomes the permeable membrane of deepest relatedness between the one and the many, the center and all centers. And in some mysterious way, it is open to a vast awareness. Here, at this paradoxical center, which by its very nature transcends all polarities, I experience the greatest intimacy with all that surrounds me.

This was the beginning of the healing of polarities, the weaving of a new relationship between self and universe. The symbol of the compass symbolizes Integrity: our embodiment of—and embeddedness within—a mysterious wisdom which may someday permit us as individuals to fly as members of the human flock, attuned to both the needs of our species and of the earth community.

⮆

These ways of discovering and relating to center were essential to my getting new bearings. Yet there is another crucial paradox having to do with center and bearing that the dream makes manifest. In an earlier age, where cyclical and seasonal time frames pertained, the symbols of mandala and journey inward "where God resided" sufficed. Now we realize that the idea of a center and a

---

* Stated more eloquently: "God is my center when I close him in and my circumference when I melt in him." Angelus Silesius (1624-1677), was a poet from Silesia (now Poland).

journey inward have a static quality which also needs to be balanced. Today we know we live in a *time-developmental* context.* The story of the universe is unfolding. It is one of continuous emergence and evolution. We are part of an open universe, not a closed one, and as such, we are also transforming and creating.

Both dreams, the one about the two concrete pillars and the one about the compass bearer, expressed this reality of constant metamorphosis. The first offered a moving river as an alternative to a static world view. The second dramatized the same truth in not one but three ways. First, the compass is presented as a means of maintaining my bearings on a *journey* along the shore. Not only will I need to stay attuned to my changing surroundings by being on center; I will be moving. Like the universe, I will be in process. By staying attuned to my process, I will be guided. Staying attuned to my process becomes a way of staying attuned to the process of all creation. Perhaps it is one and the same thing.

So I am both at center and moving. With both, I have my bearings. I am helped to accept both the static and moving aspects of center by the two theories of light. Some questions about the reality of light can be answered by a theory that says light is a particle, and others can better be answered by one that describes light as a wave. These two facts, like the sphere which whirled in two directions, cannot be reconciled within our language and knowledge structure.

The dream dramatizes metamorphosis in a second way by centering not a needle, but a spiral shell in the compass card. The spiral is a pattern found throughout evolution and throughout nature. It is a result of *growth*. With the exception of galaxies,

---

* This is a term used by Thomas Berry and developed by Brian Swimme in contrast to the idea of a static universe.

whirlpools and spiral winds, all spirals are made by living things.[1]
DNA, the very substance of life, is formed in a spiral. We see the
pattern in shells, in the arrangement of leaves around a twig and
branches about a stem. Because spirals represent continual growth,
the dreamer has chosen an apt metaphor. Our constant circling
and revisiting of the dimensions of life and death at deeper and
deeper levels is how we grow.

The third representation of the dynamic aspect of bearing is
that the journey is taking place along the shoreline. It is at the
edges between differences where things happen; not only at the
boundary of the sea and the land, but at other verges. When
native tribes meet peoples from other lands, some of the old ways
of both groups are destroyed and entirely new forms of government
(such as democracy), evolve; new crafts and new world views. The
same phenomenon of pain and growth happens between friends
and between lovers. At the interface between red and blue comes
a new color, purple. Between chemicals there are opportunities for
explosion as well as bonding. *Amidst diversity* is dynamism—and
energy. It is the energy of life's own process of destruction and
creativity in a creative and emergent universe.

And so I learned to invite differences. Very tentatively, I began
to receive and affirm the part of each opposite that I had dis-
owned. I realized that I had to enter a dualism in order to dispel it.
It helped to remember the motorcycle journey, when my husband
was dipping deep into the curves, like ribbon candy on a road.
There, the magnificent sense of freedom was created *by steering
into the fall.* That willing entry into what felt like disaster created
the exhilarating experience of the dance.

I am reminded of a dramatic example. I had flown back alone
to my small New Hampshire house one week in May for a desper-

ately needed vacation. I had looked forward to writing, hiking, exploring the terrain. Within 24 hours my plans dissolved. I woke with a terrible case of the flu—high fever, exhaustion, weakness, all the symptoms. I lay all morning on the couch, looking out into the woods, miserable and disappointed. Unexpectedly, a *sense* erupted through the weight of the fever that I should go outdoors and cut down the saplings along the stone wall. How absurd! I could barely walk, much less handle a saw. But the sense was palpable. I could feel the message: *Go cut down the trees.*

I argued with that bodily urgency for an hour. Then it occurred to me: *why not follow it?* I dragged myself to the shed, got a saw and went to tackle the first tree. I was so weak, I could barely move my arm. I pulled the saw back and forth a few strokes, then sank into the bed of dry leaves piled up alongside the stone wall. I tried again and collapsed again, persisting until the tree was felled. Then I dragged it across the stone wall through the thick brush into the woods.

Exhausted, I headed into the house for some water and fell heaving on the couch. The compelling sense returned. *Go cut down another.* How could I? Look at me? I had barely the strength to do the first. *Cut the next.* I did. Came back in the house. Drank water. Collapsed on the couch.

I did the same with the third. And the fourth. But I began to wonder. Was I imagining it? I seemed to be feeling a little bit better. I went back to the wall again. Cut the fifth. Dragged it, panting into the woods. By the end of the afternoon, all the saplings were cut, and the flu symptoms had completely disappeared! I had my strength back and my energy. Days later, I wrote a poem.

~❧

DESTRUCTION

I sawed down
twenty-five trees one day.
Watched them fall with glee
and hauled them
over the stone wall
to die.
And that's nothing
compared with what else I want to do
sometimes.

~❧

I had always loved my creativity. Now, by following a very
subtle sense from my depths, I had found my destructiveness as
well. I discovered in this way that when I was willing to be present
to the truth of the moment, however dangerous it seemed, it
became an act of embrace. As conflicting situations confronted
me, I imagined myself reaching out—first with one arm, then the
other—to both polarities and taking them into the core of my self.

It was not without a fight. But it was a beginning of making
room for the truth: about me, about others and about life. Of
bearing reality. Seeking beyond opposites like good and evil, male
and female, constructive and destructive, I discovered the resonance between them. At center, the opposites were *knit*. Instead
of being split by "knowing," they were *brought into relationship* by
invitation and acceptance.* For me, it is symbolic that I was given

---

* The Greeks have a term which describes this relationship between opposites when dualism has not split them asunder: *enantiodromia*.

a woman's compass, for bringing into relatedness is a particularly feminine faculty. That receptive embrace, as we shall see, has the greatest implications for Integrity.

The compass offered in the dream became a rich resource for my journey. It symbolized a context for an ongoing dying and rebirth. Surely the journey represented the birthing of a new identity, one which created an intimate relationship between me and the rest of creation. And its timing was impeccable: although it had not yet been widely appreciated, our world had just begun to enter what Thomas Berry has called the Ecological Age.

It would not be a surprise to me if our own inner process were indeed related to that of the earth. We are, after all, a manifestation of its spiral journey. In the outer world, the integration of nations and economies and even curriculums, as I see it, reflects our more inward journeys. There seems to be the kind of movement, so often seen in evolution, toward coalescing. Toward Integrity.

Integrity has to do with wisdom. It is a kind of "knowing together." Knowing together, as we have explored it thus far, has extended the idea of knowing with our minds to accessing a more subtle kind of wisdom that depends on letting go of those old mental categories. It depends, in part, on a vulnerability to images and to others; to feelings, to presence and to sensing. Knowing together also integrates both sides of the pairs of opposites. It is a gradual process of surrender to what I call the *Other*: to that which I do *not* know. And the unknown is ultimately that mystery which is, by definition, beyond my comprehension.

On this journey of surrender, I experienced other ways of "knowing together" that were astonishing. Perhaps the most amazing to me still, is the experience of knowing with my nature. *With nature.*

Part Three

~

An Expanding Identity

7

Dance, Wild Beast

In the context
of cosmic
values
only the
fantastic
has a chance
of being true.
                    —Teilhard de Chardin[1]

When I walk through the doors of the Monterey aquarium, I enter the world of the creature. It is an abrupt break with the fast, above-ground world of concrete freeways and steel capsules on wheels where I am estranged from my surroundings.

It is dark there, a dim underworld where kelp, swaying with the tides, towers over me like tall palm trees in the wind. In these timeless depths, schools of fish, glinting silver, slither as one body round an invisible axis. Beneath them, a black stingray undulates sensuously like a graceful bird; rough barnacles sweep their feathery fans to cup the tide; and giant squid, their tentacles churning, fasten to the glass a hundred mouths sucking like infants at breast.

Ruby-stemmed sea anemones thicker than my ankles stand crowned with a bush of graceful milky-white arms that reach in all directions like seductive dancers. Sea otters dive and roll, then float on their backs, patting their stomachs contentedly; scratching and smoothing their own dark wet fur, a satiny self caress that seemingly never ends.

Life renews itself continuously, inventively—salmon battle upstream to trade their lives for their young. Pencil-like sea sticks procreate in reverse—the females impregnate males with their eggs. Other creatures line up in chains of fertilization, one end of a body receiving sperm, the other end impregnating a partner. Millions of eggs ride helplessly on the tides, while others are tucked carefully away in encapsuled hiding places.

Crowds of South American red shrimp poise for battle, signal attack with their claws waving, then step back one pace. Rest. Repeat. The pattern is fixed. Meanwhile the salmon lazily circle, then swiftly attack their prey. Jaws snap! Done. The slick black stingray floats down like a parachute over a fish, flattens out on the sandy bottom, and in a reverse of birth, takes the fish into its hidden mouth at the center of its body. A fat sea slug tracking the slime of a snail opens its round wide mouth and slurps it in, whole. The whole luminous underwater display reeks of life: opening, seeking, closing, stinging, squirming, sucking, spewing, penetrating, erupting, sliming, slurping, chomping, spawning, biting, dying.

Erotic.

Dance, Wild Beast

~

*And I dreamed of dancing in the forest, bare to the
waist, my legs those of a hoofed animal, long and hairy,
and over my face a thick wooden mask, painted with
geometric designs.*

As I woke, I relished the bare-breasted freedom, my animal,
hairy sexuality, yet the presence of the mask in the dream told me
I was still afraid. Instead of revealing myself as I was, I tried to hide
behind something that was rigid and fabricated. Beneath the mask
was my soft wild face, my eyes, luminous in the dark. I did not
know this body-self. I felt safer, perhaps, as a balloon tied with a
string than as an erotic animal-woman,* abandoned to the dance.
Her body was vitally alive, yet her head was wood.

In waking life too, my body is *always* ahead of my head. Ever
since I struggled with the strangling sensation around my throat,
she has been a stern taskmistress. With tweaks and twinges and
aches and stabs, she's made me pay attention to things my thinker
didn't want to notice.

My body is my teacher. She tells me what I am feeling and lets
me know what I am ignoring or denying in my environment. If I
were to take pain medication, I lose these opportunities for incredible learning. And so I don't. Since I began to pay attention to my
body, countless barriers between my outer and inner self have
dissolved. Most important, my receptivity to others increases as I
become more receptive to myself. Moreover, I am more sensitive
to information coming from my environment, more open to

* I have searched for the female centaur in literature without success. However, years after
this dream, I found a Victorian table in an inn in Butte, Montana, the legs of which were
figures of naked women with deer or goat legs and cloven hooves.

93

learning from the rest of the created world. *I believe that this perme-ability is central to functioning as an integral part of the whole in the new Ecological Age,* a truth offered to me as I began to respect the wisdom of my body.

After the strangling sensations went away, I began to feel what seemed to be iron bands around my chest. They returned intermit-tently for many months. These sensations frightened me and I wondered if I would ever get a deep breath, much less be relieved of the pain. Yet when I ultimately dared to feel the honest feelings I was protecting myself from knowing, the pain vanished. As I worked to identify what was going on in me at the time, I realized that my body was (in Kunkel's words), trying to keep me "honest rather than good."

The sensations demanded my attention because they hurt. I experienced them as my body's way of teaching me the truth about who I really am. When I listened to the symptoms, I let go. I began to see my pain as a way of getting honest, of acceptance and of compassion. With the truth—that which had not fit between the concrete polarities of my identity—came an immediate cessa-tion of the pain.

The symptoms prepared my body to be the receiver I imagined on the motorcycle journey. At the same time, I began to inhabit myself more deeply; really live down into my body. In this down-ward journey, the more I *am* a body, the more I am *in* and *of* Nature. And in and of my own nature as well.

After the dream of the centaur, I had begun to feel a savage pain in my right shoulder, as if I were being stabbed in the back, a sharp invisible dagger impaled between my shoulder blade and my spine. It came and went. Nothing I did or thought or felt seemed to relieve it. In desperation, I took a walk one day, begging for relief-giving truth.

As I stormed up a long hill, I pleaded with my body, this Other whom I did not know, who spoke in a language of pain:

> *You keep at me with your stab-in-the-back-pain. For God's sake, what is it you want? I've felt everything I can feel. When will it be enough?*

I was angry and desperate. As I pressed upward, the effort eroded my self control, bringing strange sensations from far down inside me. Like the poetry when it emerged for the first time, these rising movements were without precedent. Though I was tired, I kept pushing up the hill, seeking a way to engage the sensations. Were there any words? No. Nor were there tears. Nor anger. It was clear that I had to leave logic, language and feeling behind and enter my body on its own terms. Something deeper was laboring toward the light.

> *All right! Whatever you are, I will support you...I will give you a name.*

I swept my arms wide open and surrendered to the pain:

> *Strange...not words...No...sounds...What is it? ...Feels like a ...RUH!...GRUH! ...URHAHHHHHHHHHHHHH... GRUHAAAHHHHOOOORRRRRAAAAAOOORRR!!!! RRRAAAAAAAAAAOOOOOOOOOOOOGGGHHHHHUH!*

The guttural eruptions from my mouth seemed to spew from my belly. I ground my teeth. **NNNGGNNAAAAGH!** The sensa-

95

tion was exhilarating. In my mind's eye I saw claw marks on some unknown cheeks and felt flesh under my nails. NNGGNNAAAGH! In my imagination, my claws tore at some creature's eyeballs and left bloody sockets. It felt *wonderful*. I was astonished.

Comes the beast, long held at bay, hidden under a wooden mask, dancing on animal legs, wailing the wild, wild wail.

I cried. The pain had gone.

Oh...feels good! What a relief! The dagger has melted with my tears. I'm crying in greeting.

A word explodes inside me:

SATISFYING!!

I found myself utterly quiet, calm, reflective. Spiritually naked, I turned and walked back the way I had come, knowing I had met something long lost. And the word *satisfying!* a word I had never used before, rang round and round within me. At home, I looked up its roots. It came from the Latin, *satis facere: to make full.* Satisfying to bring my beast home. Real food.

As my body is released, I am given language. An abundance of words, more exact and expressive than I have ever used before, occur to me unexpectedly. I begin to experience *language turning back on itself.* My assertion is that *language comes out of the body,* that its roots often reflect deeper truths which customary usage disguises. Customary usage can tend to suppress the original—and uncomfortable—meanings of a word by rendering them "obsolete." In this way, just as the obsolete meanings of anger are related to the bodily grief and pain of a wound, the word *satisfy* fills a wide range of meaning, from meeting our most base *animal* hungers and sexual desires to obsolete *theological* amends.

Moreover, the word *satis* has its roots in the Middle English *sad*, meaning full, sated, sad. There is a completeness to this early meaning—meaning both to render complete and to experience the sadness of that fulfillment. We satisfy a hunger or a sexual longing, then experience the energetic letdown to balance the voracity of appetite. The original word risen from the human body millennia ago did not reflect the split. We are the ones who have *decided* to limit ourselves to only one meaning.

In fact, like the swirling colors of my childhood rubber ball, "satisfy" has many more than two opposing definitions. A multitude of meanings lies between its instinctual and ecclesiastical applications. Among them: We assure or satisfy ourselves by investigating a question. We satisfy or content ourselves with moderation. We satisfy a debt owed or an equation's conditions. We perform a penitential act to satisfy church authority for an injury to another or to God.

But what about injury to ourselves? *Is it not a true injury to ourselves as we were created, to deny our very nature—our creatureliness?* The eruption of the word "satisfying!" in me, along with tears of greeting, expressed a *meeting*, a *communion* more profound than I had ever experienced at any altar rail. In being willing to support and sustain the unknown that was emerging in me, I came to have compassion for my beast, *which is my body.* In a new kind of trust and acceptance, that which had been split into opposites was knit.

❧

Shortly afterwards I found myself walking alone with a new bearing across a large ballroom in front of hundreds of strangers. As I noticed my unusual feeling of comfort in front of the crowd, I discovered to my amazement that in my body, someone was home. It was me.

❧

As a result of this experience, "bearing" developed yet another meaning for me. Bearing what was real: the tension, the violence, the beast, let me bear—*give birth to*—something new. It was not a reversion to the past. I did not become an animal or act out the violence from my ancient depths. Instead, my body and I were mutually ennobled by knowing and being known by the other. I discovered something profoundly firm in me to balance the tenderness which had previously disclosed itself. This strength was entirely different from my control. But it is unlikely that it would have emerged without that prior embodiment, the container of gentleness and compassion. One tempers—and permits—the other. The presence of the one lets the other trust itself in me. The lion can lie down because of the lamb. The lamb can lie down because of the lion. *Communion*. Out of the two, something entirely new can be born.

❧

Hatred hides
in a hollow.
Beckoned (finally)
with full embrace,
it breaks unsoftened,

rounds out
sound,
soul and sorrow.
Seeds Love.[2]

❧

By admitting, *allowing* into my awareness, my deeply encoded capacities for aggression and destruction, I experienced a new appreciation for the realities of the animal world. I, too, was red in tooth and claw, as erotic as the undersea creatures and the dancing centaur pulsing with life. But the root meaning* of erotic was also present. With greater self revelation, I found myself being born into a more intimate relationship with the beauty and mystery of the natural world as it is, without an overlay of my judgment. I found myself less separated from it. This was a great gift. But another gift was to follow.

Driving home the night I experienced that raw animal nature, six deer stood in front of my car at the main crossroad of our thickly settled suburb. In nine years, I had never seen a deer on the road. Moreover, it was spring and the rainy season, so the forests were lush and the fields green. The deer did not lack food or water. I rolled down my window and spoke to them softly, as if to warn them. They startled momentarily, then lined up in pairs in front of my car. Then, as I rolled slowly behind, high beams illuminating them like a spotlight, all six marched sedately down the center of the road, two by two, as if in harness ahead of my car, for almost a quarter of a mile.

I was entranced. I knew this was not normal animal behavior and wondered about its meaning. Society would have called it

* From the Greek *eros* meaning *love*.

coincidence. I wondered if it were not an opportunity to look at life through a wider lens. Could I keep from diminishing such joy and mystery as this—not cut it off at the boundaries of conventional definition?

I wondered at the fact that this unusual event had occurred the very day I had honored my own animal reality for the first time. What if the animal world were now acknowledging the beginnings of my willingness to be a member of its reality? Though my inner skeptic—I cherish it as important—argued with this thought, I chose to watch and continue to question my experience from this new point of view. It was the harder view to keep nourished.*

The shoulder pain was intermittent and mild after that, amenable to briefer and less dramatic insights and feelings. Then, three months later, when I was on the East coast for my daughter's marriage, it became almost unbearable again. It was five days before the wedding, and she had suggested visiting me for a quiet day in our small New Hampshire house. How I looked forward to being with her! It was an unrepeatable moment of passage. I loved her deeply and was grateful for the opportunity to mark it with her.

Still, the backstab pain had been excruciating for days and nothing seemed to relieve it. It was unremitting. Failing to assuage it, I *had* to welcome the truth—*no matter what*. It was preferable to the pain. With my daughter due at any moment, I dropped in desperation to my knees and begged:

---

* I asked Buck Ghost Horse, a medicine man of the Lakota (Sioux) tribe about my experiences. He said that deer just don't walk that way in front of cars! He went on to say that there is one spirit in all of us and that the spirit takes different forms. He said that the creatures were teaching me something, that it was good that I was letting go and that it was good that I was seeing them as teachers. He taught me how to thank them, and said they are telling us that we are not alone, that we are never alone, that we always have our companions.

Your knife-in-the-back is too deep! Look. I can't enjoy
her or be available to her in this kind of pain. She's
coming in an hour. For God's sake, what is it you want
me to know? I'll accept anything. Dammit, help me!!*

In a flash of images, I remembered the promises of my own childhood: cascading wedding bouquets and a veil of white net, a 'happily ever after ending.' I remembered walking down the aisle as a bride; giving birth and holding small children with warm flesh and velvet skin; I remembered sticky dandelion bouquets and wagons and crayon drawings of horses; birthday cakes and soft wet kisses. I had spent my entire childhood and adolescence preparing to be bride, wife and mother. And I had loved the experience.

Now it was over. I was no longer young.

In my mind's eye I saw my daughter enter the church in her exquisite size six wedding dress. Her skin was luminous, her blond hair drawn up from the nape of her neck. She started down the same aisle where I had stood as a young mother when I was exactly her age. I remembered the times I'd watched her toddle down that aisle to greet her father at the organ bench after every Sunday service. As the people in my mind crowded forth to see her bridal procession, unexpected sounds exploded from my lips in a shriek:

You! How DARE you push me off into the wings!!!

My eyes bulged in disbelief. I was horrified. Whose voice was it? I did not know. I would not have believed such wrath was within me, but my body told me differently:

---

* It was during this spiritual journey that I learned that prayers in the trenches can be a lot different from those in the prayerbook!

101

*Oh, relief! The pain is gone. I know you now, old hag
…The tears feel good as I greet you…And the same
word is reverberating in my body again:*

SATISFYING!

It was humbling to admit such a personage into my self. Yet unquestionably, she lived in me, fully drawn. How could I not receive this thirteenth fairy* who had been left out for so long? Had I not needed to learn repeatedly to welcome into my center the lost portions of my soul? The ugly? The homeless? Eight years before, when I had just begun the "journey down," my first dream image had been of a witch chasing me through a maze. At the time I had been terrified. Now I knew she had been searching to find a home. I reached out to the one who had been unlovable and took her in.

How far back her voice goes—back into the shadows of the human race! In it were the wild and untamed intonations present in females since the beginning of time, part of our grieving. I understood what my body had been telling me with the backstab pain. I had been shouldering the collective unconscious of my species, denying a very real part of my identity. *There are so many more selves in me than I would have believed.* All—among them the tender child, the beast and the hag—are satisfying because they have completed me. I am made full.

I gathered the laundry and took it out to the car. There was just time to get to the laundromat before my daughter arrived. As I rolled down the hill from my house, I began to smile as I imagined a new name for the inner personage I'd just met: "the swamp

---

* In fairy tales, the thirteenth fairy was the one who was not invited to the baptism, and furious at being left out, appeared anyway with a curse for the child to be effected when the child turned adolescent.

goddess." Just then, a huge, many-pointed buck arced across the road in front of my car. It was 11:40 A.M. Never had I seen a deer there on the land in fourteen years. Though they clearly were abundant in the woods, they had many predators (including man), and it was very unusual for a deer to show itself on a road at that hour in the morning. Again I experienced it as a confirmation, remembering Buck Ghost Horse's words. I was at peace.

Five minutes after I returned from the laundromat, my daughter arrived. My love for her and my ability to be present to her had considerably deepened. The pain did not return. Several days later, my joy was unbounded as I danced at her wedding—without a mask.

Over the next year, deer appeared at significant times in my life at least eight times. Each sighting was preceded by the stab-in-the-back pain. Within a split second of accepting the spontaneous feelings of my beast—my primal woman—a single deer had appeared. I still find this simultaneity astonishing. If I *thought about* deer in conjunction with what was going on in my mind or body, one never appeared. Only as a complete surprise did I experience this synchronicity. Then the phenomenon stopped and I began to see patterns in the unusual behavior of other species as well.

Nevertheless, at home two years later, I was walking my dog in a state of reverie, recalling the time I had been on my knees in New Hampshire. As I felt the flood of feeling again, there was a sharp tug on the leash. I looked up just in time to see a stag leaping across the road not fifteen feet ahead.*

* At 1 A.M., the night I mailed this chapter to Brian Swimme for review, I encountered five deer in the same place I first saw them in my suburb. It was a year to the date that I had first encountered them.

I do not understand such events. They don't yield easily to logical explanation. We humans have tended to be convinced that what we see is what the world is. For many centuries, our culture has dismissed as "magical thinking" what it cannot understand or logically codify. There is a kind of hubris in assuming that we can take the measure of reality.

Let there be magic! How many ways there are of encountering the universe—what richness these experiences lend to life! What meaning!

I have continued to test ways of expanding my reason to include these intersecting realities. I am helped by Jung's theory of synchronicity which he defines as "an acausal connecting principle."[3] Jung also confirms that "a new attitude is created, an attitude which accepts the non-rational and the incomprehensible *simply because it is happening.*"[4]

I accepted the repeated appearance of the deer at moments of meaningful integration as a 'Yes!' from the community of life, a confirmation.* Whether or not my associations between bodymind and nature are "true" cannot be assessed because proof requires duality.† What matters to me is how I *used* that synchronicity to allow other aspects from the darkness to be woven into the tapestry of who I am. I used that interpretation to

---

* This was reinforced in 1990, five years after the experience, when I found a quote referring to "...the psychoid level of consciousness where the animal roots of the soul have their origins... (Hermes') association with the psychoid level establishes synchronicity as a link between the world of the mind and the world of matter. This level is the very ground of being, the *unus mundus*, the meeting place of mind and nature... From this deep well synchronicity draws its meaning, so that each synchronistic coincidence mirrors the same significance in the world of objective matter as in the world of inner experience." Allan Combs and Mark Holland, *Synchronicity: Science, Myth and the Trickster* (New York: Paragon House, 1990), pp. 142-143.

† See discussion about the issue of proof which follows in chapter 8.

encourage myself on a journey which was increasingly frightening. I had been terrified of the beast, the prowling, growling one in the depths of my paleolithic consciousness.* Yet deer expressed many other facets of wildness which were essential to me. They knew how to protect and defend themselves. At the same time, they demonstrated vulnerability and beauty, spontaneity and poise, curiosity and grace. I wanted to think this combination was also hiding behind the wooden mask of this dancing animal-woman.

Each of us is a creature, not just an ego. One needs to be a *body* to be one among many. Our thinking and knowing *rests* on this foundation. *Embodied*, we are kin to the beings around us— animals and trees, stones and stars. It is a profound relatedness, acknowledged through our bodies—our beasts.

Our beasts squirm and spew, smell and secrete. They live. And, being animals, they die. By forgiving and accepting my beast, I reclaim realities long lost when knowledge began to be disembod- ied. As I bond once again with the tangible earthy reality, my body receives the subtle signals that had formerly been blocked by *knowing*. I turn to the center and embrace this ancient but new-to- me kind of understanding *along with logic*. That shared knowledge is a wisdom of being.

Until I greeted that which I feared (like the dark tarantula and bull on the motorcycle journey), I was unable to embody the hidden strength or beauty of wildness. Wild myself, I could now be fully present to the wilderness. It became an entirely new experi-

---

* After this chapter had been completed, I spent two weeks in the Alaskan wilderness where bear and other wild creatures rule, and was reminded of John McPhee's quoting a native Alaskan: "If you're going to get et, you're going to get et," in *Coming into the Country* (New York: Farrar, Straus and Giroux, 1977), p.283. We humans have worked for millen- nia to leave behind this law of reality: *who is eating whom*. So doing, we have also left behind a huge portion of ourselves—our bodies and the wisdom inherent in them for sur- viving in such an environment.

ence of intimacy with the earth community. It meant that I was vulnerable to the world.

Genuine intimacy requires presence to what is happening about me. Nature can no longer be merely a backdrop for my activities. I need to enter into the natural world and allow it to affect my soul. Such moments of presence and intimacy between self and any Other can result only when there is mutual self disclosure. It seems that when creatures reflect one another in truth, they explode the myth of otherness. In the kinds of examples I have chosen, the dynamism between intersecting realities calls all of our "knowing" into question. Surely we are talking about something profound that cannot be contained or expressed in the way we usually think—in the customary polarization between animal and human, thought and event, psyche and viscera.

From yet another perspective, reality cannot be seen and defined by just one species. The perceptions of a hawk, a bee, a fawn, a bacterium in the soil, are different from our own, and in each case more sensitive in some ways than we are. Reality is more like an interpenetrating of consciousnesses. It can only show itself in the community of being,[5] in "the fullness thereof." *Such a radical humility is absolutely essential for our time.*

This deep relatedness between life's varied manifestations represents a kind of healing with implications for all of us, mending the web of which we are all a part. *The larger identity we need is formed not alone and not in an isolated nuclear family, but here.* I call this relatedness Integrity—an *ecological identity.*

~●

Underneath, an inner voice speaks:

106

I drop the wooden mask and am ordained by my body. I receive the world and am received in return. I taste and laugh and leap and love and never forget that I die today and tomorrow and forever. Tenderness and wildness and wonder rise in me and I begin to care. Everything has become sacred. I find myself speaking love and feeling terror at being so out of control.

And another voice whispers:

I will show you love. Alive, down in the loamy richness of my body, I am earth and all of her display. I wear talons forged in the fire. I will protect you fiercely—and abandon myself like the cherry blossom as it lets go the branch and flutters to the green meadow.

8

The Languages of the Cosmos

We impose control to free us from our fears of chaos,
but this seeming chaos in us is a rich, rolling, swelling,
dying, lilting, singing, laughing, shouting, crying,
sleeping **order**.
—Paraphrased from Christopher Alexander[1]

Reason collided with experience and the life force exploded in my body, leaving every cell trembling. Overwhelmed by the energy that was released, I imagined my body expanding to contain it. Something grew. Although I didn't understand it then, in time I'd realize my identity had expanded: *who I am*.

Though I recognized the aliveness was positive, I knew I needed a resting place, and turned out of habit to reason. What amazed me was a gift of *form*, form that gave shape to my experiences and lent respite from the confusion. Quite unexpectedly, an image whirled into my imagination: the toddlers' stacking toy, a graduated pyramid of six colored "donuts" floating in space without its center post. (See Figure 2.) It shimmered like a rainbow-colored satellite, a small red donut at the top, a large violet one at the bottom, the rest of the spectrum in between. Tipped on its axis, the top of the pyramid had one side facing a distant sun. That upper left side was brightly lit, its colors clear, its surfaces crisp. The side away from the sun was in a shadow which darkened by degrees as it swept down the pyramid's rings until it completely engulfed the largest ones at the base.

Because of the light's angle, the top four rings were half in shadow. Inscribed on the brightly lit side of the top red ring was *"language"* and on its shadowed side, *"image."*

On the bright side of the next ring which was orange, was inscribed *"emotion"* and on its darker side, *"feeling."* On the yellow ring below that was written *"sensing"* and on its more shadowed side, *"instinct."* The green fourth ring was hazier and less clearly divided. Its brighter side held the words *"the shamanic"* and the darker, *"dream."* The entire fifth ring was in deep shadows. On its deep blue surface was printed *"intuition."* At the base, color and outline barely discernible, the darkest violet ring held the words *"the unfolding story of the cosmos."*

Black space surrounded the structure and filled the hollow axis on which it spun like a jewelled top. On that space five words curved around the image like an embrace:

mystery—the creative—the void

Direction of most control:
Information is the most limited, isolated and incongruent with the whole.

Area of
rational analysis,
decision-making,
"ordinary
communication"

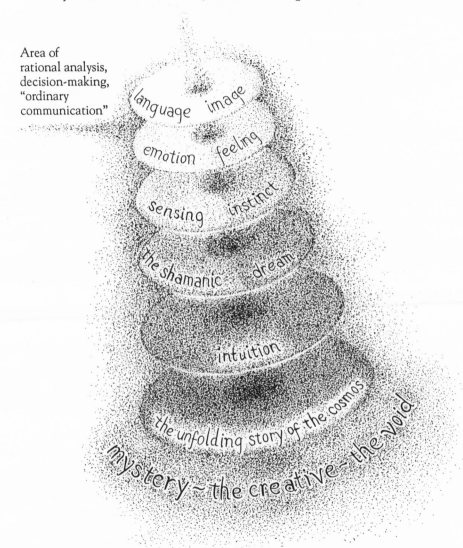

Direction of most vulnerability:
*Access to the greatest degree of wisdom, autonomy, creativity
and integration with the whole.*

Figure 2

The rings seemed almost to hum with one another, as if resonant parts of a chord. The only thing that apparently held them
together was that harmony—and the emptiness at the core, the
void.

The image appeared to me as a complete form—an unexpected
gift. It offered me a temporary sense of order whenever I felt most
confused. As a toy, it honored the child part of me. I was not
unmindful that it was the toddler in me who first enjoyed toys that
created order. Moreover, I knew I could leave this toy behind
when I was through playing, and return to the immediacy of each
day.*

The words on the rings had caught my interest. While I'd
taken my intellect along on the journey thus far, I'd needed to
quiet it to hear the languages of image, feeling, instinct and dream.
Now I felt the excitement of new ideas taking hold. Logic wanted
to play.

The pyramid of rings was like a map of the conscious descent I
had taken, plunging deeper into subjective experience and, conse-
quently, deeper into the mysteries of the cosmos. Reflecting, I
remembered two other images of descent: the road sign pointing
'one way' in a dream, and the motorcycle journey down the dark
side of Mt. Hamilton. On the back of the motorcycle, I had flung
my arms wide, imagining a huge satellite dish and exclaimed
"That's who we really are—living, breathing receivers!" As I
looked at this new image, I recognized that the colored rings
represented languages within me that I had been learning to
receive: languages that greatly amplified for me what it meant to
be a human being.

---

* For me, this is an essential attitude to take toward any theory!

At the top were the symbolic languages of the culture: languages of word (or number) and image (or symbol) we learn as children from the adults who tell us who we are. Beneath them were the more personal languages of emotion and feeling, languages not limited to our species, lying deeper in our souls. Below those, were the rings representing the languages of the natural world: sensing and instinct, the shamanic, the dream and intuition. Shared with our ancient forbears and the animal world, these languages are etched deep in our genes. Even more profoundly, inscribed in our beings are the languages of our royal heritage: the majesty of the story of the cosmos and the mystery out of which it emerged.

I called this model The Languages of the Cosmos. It represents *story* with the action stopped. It is an ordering of my descent, and orders the chapters of this book, as well. The model is a stylized helix, a spiral, one of nature's primal forms. It symbolizes a journey of receptivity to greater and greater nuance; one in which we recognize a human identity far richer than the one our culture acknowledges. Each turn of the spiral reflects a deeper integration and healing. Seen as a pyramid of rings with Mystery at its core, it expresses an alternative way of being in the world.

If we look at the model as a whole, we can see that the languages on the lighted portions of the left side are more accessible, easier for us to control, and lend themselves to our own initiative and effort. Those on the right have more of a life of their own— they're more spontaneous. They also carry more information than the corresponding languages to the left. If we proceed downward through the languages, moving from the light to the dark side of each ring, the first thing we encounter is image. We already know that a picture is worth a thousand words. We are also aware of the importance of imagery in the creative act, in science[2] as well as literature. Imagery enriches metaphor and is at the heart of symbol and ritual. We also associate it with healing. Treatments for cancer and other diseases now often include *both* traditional medicine *and* visualization.

We humans had mental imagery long before we had spoken or written language. *To use imagery today is an act of healing, integrating our current mode of thinking with older languages and mental processes from our evolutionary heritage. I believe that as images and the other shadowed languages are knit up into our lives, we are healed even more deeply—first within ourselves, and then in our relationship with all that surrounds us.*

Many people in western culture never go beyond the language of words, even to explore the wisdom found in imagery. Even fewer seek the next ring—that of their own feelings. Feelings are our body's authentic responses to life. For me, they are a powerful language in a truer, more transformative sense than words, because they are indicators for self change. Feelings tell me the truth. Honestly assessed and *combined with* thought, they provide a more moral basis for our logical decisions.

I would like to tell some personal stories of healing which happened quite unexpectedly as I became receptive to images, feelings and instincts. They are descriptions of experiments I have made in my life and are not offered as solutions. Too often after someone discovers a way to respond to illness in a non-traditional way, our culture tries to turn it into an Answer. The idea of a Method negates life's own creativity. Each of us is a part of that creativity, and therefore by definition, a creator. Our creativity is important, particularly *the act of making a creative response to our own situation in life.*[3]

One evening I had come down quite suddenly with a miserable cold. I was feverish and sick. That day I had built up a good-sized resentment directed at my husband, George. He was flying in from a long business trip and I discovered he had made plans—weeks before—to go out to dinner that night with some buddies. Problem was, he had neglected to tell me about these plans, and I'd accidentally found out about them through his friend the day before. I didn't like it one bit.

After his plane had landed, he had come and gone like a whirlwind. I sat alone in bed surrounded by Kleenex boxes and hot tea, quite out of sorts. It was six P.M. I began to wonder why I had such a cold. It had been rare for me, in the past 13 years, to get sick. As I began to listen to my body, the honest feeling rose. I wasn't just angry at George, I felt absolutely murderous! It was that damned swamp goddess in me again! In part, I realized I had ignored my anger because George was flying home. For obvious reasons, waiting for him to arrive from a flight triggers old memories and I become very vulnerable. But in addition, I find it just plain hard to admit feelings of anger about anyone I love. Then a new question rose from that strange, mystical part of my mind that feels larger than me: *could not love contain anger?* When George came home at ten o'clock, I'd put the Kleenex boxes away and my cold symptoms were entirely gone. I had taken no medication. He was astonished at the change in just four hours. So was I.

~

Three years ago I sprouted large square arthritis "blooms" on two joints in my left hand. Doctors could not help. After weeks of trying diet and exercise to no avail, I asked my body what was going on. I knew that arthritis ran in my family and that it accom-

115

panied aging. Past fifty, I was in the midst of facing the many realities of getting older. My face was getting lined. My body needed more than moisturizer.

And so I began the difficult and often painful work of accepting aging honestly. I also felt that, for me, arthritis was a metaphor for a growing rigidity in my body and my mind. I decided to try two disciplines. I began Hatha Yoga for my body. But I also worked hard to become a more flexible person. Something happened. In the past three years, the arthritis has receded and the blooms have almost entirely vanished. Most important, both joints are still flexible. Other members of my family have large calcifications in those same joints of the left hand and cannot bend their fingers.

I don't know if these actions had anything to do with the receding arthritis. There were, perhaps, other factors well beyond my awareness. But somehow, in my way of viewing things, I wonder if there wasn't some relationship between the healing of my arthritis and a *both/and* response. Just as in the incident with George, when I found that love and hate could coexist, there was in this case *both a yes and a no* to growing older: a yes in my acceptance of aging and a no to the rigidities which I can do something about.

In the same vein, I remember when my friend's son was killed a few years ago in an automobile accident. Shortly afterwards I walked my grief up a steep hill and raged at God. "What a lousy way to run a world!" I shouted. The inner response was rapid. *How else?* As I began to explore the truth of that response, it continued with a mystic phrase: *The creative and destructive, one movement, the flame in the center of the silence.*

I offer one last example of an inclusive approach to healing. Two years ago, I stood with a hose watering some outdoor plants. Intent on my work, I stepped back—and right into a freshly dug hole for a new shrub. It felt like the earth being pulled out from under me. I fell to the ground backwards, with no time to buffer my fall, hitting my head and shoulder with full force on a concrete walk behind me. As I lay on the cement with pain shooting through my body, I started, instinctively, to tighten and push the pain away—to resist it. Then something entirely new occurred to me: *Just take the pain in. Receive it.* I lay there momentarily and imagined opening myself to the searing hurt. After a few minutes I got up, still sore, and walked into the house. My body bruises easily, and in the past I would have had quite an egg on my head. This time, there was no swelling, no bleeding, no bruising anywhere, not that day or the next; nor was there pain. I have repeated the experiment many times since with other bumps and sprains, with a similar response from my body.

~

What are the relationships between being receptive to the shadowed languages within and healing? The languages of image, feeling and instinct are distinct capacities from our evolutionary history. So is the choice to accept realities which, in our more "modern" thinking, have gotten split off: hatred, aging, death and pain. Perhaps there is a relationship between the compassionate redemption of these human attributes within us and the life force itself. I have learned repeatedly through such experiences to embrace my deeper self as *thou.* True compassion begins with ourselves. How could we be compassionate toward another and feel superior, a "helper?" We share the same swamp goddess (among others), in our ancestral souls! *We are already one among many inside.*

117

Together, the Languages of the Cosmos which I'd so clearly imagined as a pyramid of floating rings, *form an ecology, not a hierarchy.* That ecology expresses an intricate set of relationships between ourselves and our environment. As we become receptive to the language of sensing, our empathy begins to extend not only to our own kind but to all creatures. *This is the core issue for the Ecological Age.* When our identity becomes rooted in the body, we gain a new kind of intimacy with our surroundings. We may have had isolated experiences of sensing before, but now it informs us repeatedly. We "sense" the idea of a policeman just before we look in the rear view mirror and see a cop on our tail. We "know" to slow down on a curve, just before an obstruction on the road comes into view. We walk someplace in pitch dark and our feet lead us without tripping. We walk barefoot where sharp pebbles or acorns are scattered, yet never step on a one *because* we are not looking!

I believe these are gifts from our inner, animal heritage. We "know them in our bones," yet I, at least, am not aware of any sensations or other overt clues. I am reminded of my dog sleeping at the back of the house, who knows when his German shepherd "enemy" is about to pass and tears to the front room, barking ferociously. Or Farley Mowat's story, in *Never Cry Wolf*, of the Eskimos' advance awareness of when and where the caribou are arriving.

When we become receptive to these unspoken, unfelt signals from our environment, we develop an intimacy with it. The more I *am* a body (this is different from *having* a body), the more I am receptive to these languages from my surroundings! *These subtle languages are our former habitat.* We knew them *as ourselves* long before "the trees left us and we found ourselves standing upright in a savannah."[4] The more I *am* nature, the more I experience it as my *self*, the more I care for that self as *thou*. The more I care, the more responsible I am in my actions and choices which might impact it. *This is the beginning of an Ecological Identity.*

Conversely, the more I have had to learn to control my body in the civilizing process, the more its languages have fallen into disregard and disuse; and the more separate I feel from the community of life around me. The more I am lonely.

What a temptation it is to see these things in black and white, to make instinct right and control wrong, body central and mind peripheral! I have learned the importance to healing of a both/and world view. I have become particularly grateful, in this process, for the faculties of logic and judgment, the ability to *decide*. Even as I accept opposites, I also need to discern. It is an *uncertain* process, a paradox.

As I turn from sensing to the more shaded language of instinct, I move deeper into my body. I become aware of descending into my entrails. The painful backstab—the demands of my body to accept my nature—culminated in such subtle, visceral promptings that I could not even give them a name. All I could offer was my willingness to receive and support what was emerging from my depths. The wild sounds and bloody images which arose left no doubt in me that I was also a growling beast and a naked *homo habilis* woman of the savannah. Embracing that, I *am* body. And I am rooted in the larger Body that is all of us. Bringing my beast home is a spiritual feast. Having begun the journey in loneliness and despair, I celebrate my belonging.

My experience of membership in the whole corresponds to the evolving story of life. Because we are a product of the earth, the

Languages of the Cosmos reside both within us and without. The pyramid of rings is a holographic model, relating our identity to the whole of which we are a part.

Each ring builds on the levels beneath it. Instinct preceded emotion in our evolutionary history. Feeling preceded intellect.* The form which human life itself has taken rises out of and depends on those forms which preceded it. In our focus on work, relationships, politics and entertainment, we forget how utterly dependent we are on prior species, on the rhythm of planets, on gases formed at the beginning of time, on ancient bacteria in our cells, on the plants and animals which today provide us with breath and sustenance. On light, which is represented by the model's spectrum of colors.†

It is toward this majestic web of reality that the rainbow-colored Languages of the Cosmos model points. Like the greater information-carrying capacity of the violet end of the visual spectrum, the lowest violet ring represents the greatest breadth, reality and inclusiveness of language. (Beyond visible color and form, at the deepest level of mystery and the creative there lies an even greater wisdom and integration.) Conversely, the red topmost ring—like the red end of the spectrum—contains the most limited, fragmented information. Indeed, this least inclusive language, where we *decide*, is often employed without much concern for the Other—in oneself or another person, group or species. Or for the Earth. And so any problem-solving limited to

---

* While it would be difficult, empirically, to order the languages of dream and intuition within the cosmic story, intuitively I perceive them in the order presented by the Languages of the Cosmos model.

† I continue to be astonished by the complexity I have discovered in this model. It was not an intellectually created map; rather it was *given*: a complex image, perceived all at once and only later analyzed.

120

this ring tends to result in an isolated, unintegrated "solution" which fails to gain the solid and nurturing grounding of the whole system.

Thus I discovered the first paradox in this most paradoxical of images: *a person who functions primarily at the top level has the least true autonomy. At the same time, this person creates ideas and actions that are the least integrated with the needs of the rest of culture, self and nature.* A basic truth of the model, therefore, is: *One is most autonomous when one is most integrated with the whole.*

My symbol for this paradoxical state of autonomy and integration is that of the compass in the dream at Point Lobos. It consisted of a ring with a center. I didn't realize until I was finishing this book, that the compass symbol was a cross section of the rings in the Languages of the Cosmos model. Even the pyramid of rings itself is a more complex version of the spiral shell centered in that dream compass. Wherever these symbols originated, they were already deeply integrated with one another.

I discovered other paradoxes as I examined the model from the perspective of my own descent: The topmost ring represents the most familiar and accessible form of language; the bottom ring, the rarest and most elusive. As I circled subjective experience, descending through these languages, I gave up increasing degrees of comfort and apparent clarity. At the same time, I experienced more truth about myself, a process that brought increased vulnerability and, not incidentally, pain. I realized that to the extent I *expressed* these life experiences, the more I opened myself to humiliation in this culture. This is especially true for the languages at the right side of the diagram, and the phenomenon increases as one descends. How easily can we express feelings at the office; or suggest to a doctor that a dream we've had prompted us to call up and request an appointment? How often do we dare publicly voice our sensings or intuitions? How comfortable do you think I was, writing the chapter about the deer for publication?

This potential for humiliation has particular implications for the wounded child in all of us and gives us some clues about why it is so difficult to "become as little children" or seek a "beginner's mind." Much of our socialization idealizes the adult—and consists of limiting, judging, indeed crushing the child's perceptions and spirit. This has been the price paid for the kind of consciousness the human race in western culture has developed. To reclaim the habitat of the child, not only are personal pain, humiliation and increased alienation from the dominant culture involved, but our conventional world view is increasingly shattered by the experience, leaving us bereft of certainty. This was the second paradox of the model: *the mature adult is also a child. With that integration, both the potential for autonomy and creativity,* **and** *the potential for vulnerability and humiliation, increase.*

Looking at the rings one by one, I realized that the narrowest top ring represented the language over which I had the most control. Yet I had discovered that while the languages of culture give the illusion of control over life by providing distinctions, it also fragments, thereby sacrificing wisdom. Our culture excels at this kind of communication. The intellect is considered by many to be the highest accomplishment of humankind. But "high" compared to what? This is the third paradox of the model: *The less control, the more power. In other words, the more one lets go of control and trusts the other languages, the greater is the likelihood that one may begin to experience attunement with a larger order where genuine power resides.* The great paradoxes of autonomy and relatedness, humility and power, and letting go and control, are graphically resolved in this model. The more intimately we are drawn into relationship with our selves and our surroundings, the more these opposites dissolve into one another.

❧

The development of our human intellect over the millennia has required intense focus, effort *and the sublimation of the other levels of language in our socialization*. That same top-down psychological control has evolved into our social, political, religious, economic and organizational forms. They are linked through their common origin.* Some have been quick to call this origin patriarchal when it more likely has had to do with human intellectual and ego development. These are not bad things!

Now, however, those languages which have been controlled and subdued for so long need to be redeemed. At some level, our culture has recognized this need and in the last forty years, many social controls have been released. Our predicament is that the control mechanisms which have held together our institutions and buttressed our societies for centuries have dissolved *without another kind of order in place*. This is at the root of much of the political, social and economic chaos of our era—not to speak of the devastation wreaked on our psyches.

If we look at just one of our institutions, we can see an example of the disastrous results of this loosening of social control without a comparable development of inner stability in its citi-

---

* Eric Jantsch calls this growth from a common origin an "homologous form of evolution." He explores homology as one characteristic of a self-organizing system. The Languages of the Cosmos is a self-organizing system of the kind he describes in his book: *The Self-Organizing Universe* (Oxford: Pergamon Press, 1980). The book is an expanded version of the Gaither Lectures in Systems Science given in May, 1979 at the University of California, Berkeley.

zens—a stability that is rooted more deeply in the self than a choice to obey (or defy) authority:

When I was in public school in the '40s and '50s, the kinds of discipline problems our teachers addressed were pretty simple. They included talking or being 'fresh,' running when we should walk, being disruptive, and gumchewing; sometimes we were reprimanded for creating class distractions at the pencil sharpener or pushing and shoving in line; but most of the time, unless we wrote on the desks or passed notes in music class, we were not reprimanded.

Now, however, in the '80s and '90s, teachers are confronted by an appalling array of far more threatening problems: sexual behavior that includes rape, abortion and the transmission of life-threatening venereal disease; rampant drug and alcohol abuse; and physical violence—to themselves as well as their students—ranging from vandalism, extortion and robbery to assault, shootings, arson, bombings and murder.

What horror we feel as we read those words! Scenes such as these from the world of schoolchildren are vivid reminders of our crumbling order. No wonder many people yearn for the stability they once knew!

That stability was grounded in control, a mechanism which worked in psyche and society for a long period of time but with devastating results for our souls; and for our relationships to one another and to our planet. *Ours is a relative consciousness.* Until we can accept that relativity and learn to become more referent to the whole, our decisions will continue to be based on an old order which is no longer functional.

The model of the Languages of the Cosmos honors a different and more profound order: one slowly emerging in human awareness. It is the order that underlies life itself. It governs healing, honors life *and* death, creation *and* destruction, prehistory *and* the present. We cannot control, comprehend or contain it with our subject-object consciousness.

The slow emergence of this order in human consciousness reflects the measured way that life evolves. *We* cannot *do* it. But we can be receptive to hints of it in our lives, honoring *both* the old ways *and* the mystery of the new.

The Languages of the Cosmos represent *a process* toward an integrated order which respects this need for gradual change. The top ring is like a staging area from which to listen to the other levels of language. The process reminds me of a Japanese management practice that I used in my consulting, called a *Rinji* document. This is a document containing an important question to which top management wants a response. The question is amplified and embellished as it is circulated down through the layers of managers, supervisors and workers to the very "bottom" of an organization. Then the responses, beginning with the hourly workers, are brought back up through the ranks, each one adding to the comprehensive perspective which management seeks.

To use another image, the process is like using a crochet hook to reach down and pick up a dropped stitch. Just as one weaves the stitch back up through the "run" and secures it at the top, so one reintegrates the lost languages of the soul into one's self. The journey is made by reaching down into the darkness. It requires an immense faith in the unknown; but afterwards, each bit learned from deeper levels is brought up to the light to be tested against experience—and against other trusted sources.

Paradoxically, the most trusted source is the whole, the mystery toward which one keeps turning, the unknown to which one surrenders again and again. This is a spiritual* journey, not an intellectual one. Indeed, for many spiritual traditions, *seeing* is an important goal. In the process that I experienced (and probably in those other traditions, too), one must not only see but feel, sense, hear, dare, risk, hurt and fall!

❧

How shall we learn to live as one among many?

If we are to belong; if we are to respond creatively to the realities we share with the rest of creation, we need to become receptive to all of the Languages of the Cosmos. The universe requires a species made up of *individuals who are increasingly aware of all that is within them* so that they may base their decisions on *internal data* which resonates with the whole. Like the flocking birds, the collective result would be a higher group awareness and intelligence, based on choices that come from within each member.

This level of human development reaches beyond control. It requires us to be receptive to *both* the languages of human culture *and* the languages of nature. In a nutshell, we are talking about *consciously attempting to integrate the natural and the cultural within the experience of the personal.* Most important, the personhood which results is an extension of the universe in all its mystery.

This model which whirled into my awareness represented experience, something I had *done*. It seems to me that one of the

---

* Spiritual, not religious, the latter having to do with formal systems of beliefs and practises which unite their adherents in a community. For example, *in the days before human beings had words, I believe* **language** *was spiritual.*

difficulties in learning to live as one among many, is a lack of *experience* of our relatedness to the rest of the creation. Toddlers learn how the parts of this stacking toy are related from direct experience: they touch, feel, smell and taste the different colored donuts. They take them apart and place them on the stacking post repeatedly until the pieces all finally fit. They learn the relationship of the different parts to the whole. If we are to learn to function as parts of the whole, then it would seem that some growing portion of the human race must wean itself from cultural definitions of Truth in order to *experience* the connectedness of all things.

What needs to be nurtured and developed in us so that human beings can evolve into a species whose first response is for the preservation of the entire ecological community? It is tempting to respond to this question with abstractions such as love, caring, justice and compassion. Such answers are too easy. They have been preached for centuries with no appreciable change in human culture. The prior question is: How are those qualities to be generated?

In a culture of control, the spiritual journey is one of letting go.[5] For me, the journey down through the Languages of the Cosmos was a gradual letting go of judgment and control in the interest of honesty and truth. My letting go of culture and conventional views was like lifting a blind on a window to reveal the vast beauty of a landscape beyond. It was years later that I read a statement by Matthew Fox: "Spirituality, the act of waking up, is an act of resisting the boundaries and edges that society has given us…the act of making the marginal central."[6] To make culture and its creations wrong is not the intent of this book. Still, in the context of the breadth and depth of our evolutionary story, culture is a

127

narrow and limited reality. It is like looking through a tiny crack in a wall at a very narrow slice of life. Fox also says that Otto Rank "believed that the Greek quest for soul reached the summit (and its demise) when the soul was localized with the head..." He quotes Rank as saying "'Then indeed, the culture culminated. Everything that was chthonian and animal was banished to the depths...'"[7]

Integrity, then, comes about as we develop qualities and sensitivities our culture has shunned. The result is a healing, wholing* of ourselves.

As integrity evolves, we *whole* our relationships with the rest of creation. I believe that by becoming receptive to the deeper levels of being within us, we become more *attuned to that same dimension of reality outside ourselves.* I propose that, together, the inner and the outer comprise a *ring of being.* Let me give some examples. At the intellectual level of the first ring, we are all familiar with the "idea whose time has come." Again and again, inventions and movements in science and in social philosophy seem to pop up simultaneously all over the globe. We may have had a new idea ourselves and then discovered it publicized by someone else. Or it may happen the other way around. Scientists compete to bring similar ideas "to market" first. How is it that these ideas emerge at the same time?

At the level of the second ring, we are aware that by becoming receptive to feelings, we become empathic with others. We reach out with our hearts and know another's feelings. At the same time, we also often get similar feedback: others respond to us. I am suggesting that in some unexplainable way, as we become more

---

* Heal, from the Middle and Old English *hale* and its derivatives, meaning variously whole, hale, healthy and to make well.

healed at one level of language, we also make a deeper connection "outside" ourselves, at the same level; and when we do, we sometimes receive a response at that level of reality from "outside".* Suppose, then, that each ring represents *that same autonomous level of being (or its potential), in other persons and creatures.* We can then see how the model might express these levels of being throughout creation.†

Looking at the Languages of the Cosmos in this light, might it be possible that the more I trust my instinct—my beast—to inform me, the more I am subtly integrated into a new order? A ring of being with animal life? Were my experiences with the deer some kind of animal feedback?! At the level of logic, it seems preposterous, yet the important attitude for me here is to remain open to question—to novelty—rather than to solidify an answer. •

As we establish a relationship with the Other, the *thou*, in this way—at a deeply felt level of experience—we gain greater and greater autonomy. We discover things about our universe and ourselves which prove over time to be a reliable foundation for a genuine morality—one far more broadly based, and far more workable, than the black and white, right/wrong ethic we pres-

---

* Eric Jantsch describes the dynamics of a multi-level reality: "Each level maintains a certain autonomy...and lives...in horizontal relationship with its specific environment." *The Self-Organizing Universe*, p. 16.

† Brian Swimme suggested that this idea may be close to ideas in physics where an order connects disparate beings. From a personal communication, January, 1988.

• Jantsch states that the self-organizing system is not a control hierarchy but a dynamic structure. In it, cause and effect, sequential and linear time are suspended and "a state is generated (in) which...events are no longer connected in a sequential mode, but in an associative mode" with earlier events of the same basic type. *The Self Organizing Universe*, p. 302.

The issue of *time* is a huge one, one that has fascinated many besides Jantsch, Einstein and Jung. It enters into all the levels of this model and is mentioned briefly in the discussions of dream and intuition. Time is also an important dimension of the more allegorical experiences in the introduction and the coda.

ently know. Human ethics might then take their place alongside truths about one's own being in *nature*. Slowly, *our individual decisions become more integrated with the needs of all living things.*

Central to the process of the spiritual journey is a movement from control to increased autonomy.* This autonomy is grounded in an intimacy with the rest of creation *as self and as thou*—one and the same. *This state of being is the Ecological Identity, the integration of psyche and nature. It is what I mean by Integrity.*

How can these assertions be proved? They can't. The very concept of "proof" implies a duality: that which is uncertain needs to be authorized by that which is certain. But in matters of great intimacy duality dissolves. Can one "prove" he or she is really in love? I would propose a different measure. Do people who are on this journey, who follow a path beyond the boundaries, show a greater tolerance? (For they must show tolerance toward themselves if they are to face truths about who they are.) Do they demonstrate a greater capacity for compassion? (For they must forgive themselves as they stumble onto components of their own reality.) Do they seem to have increased their capacity to love, to experience more empathy with persons and nations and creatures who are different? (For they are more likely to tolerate differences once they have recognized the Other-in-themselves.) Do they translate these characteristics into service? *Whom or what do they serve?*

❧

As we descend through the rings of the model, each ring becomes larger, more prominent. The *ring of being* at each level is

---

* This movement toward autonomy is central to Jantsch's model of self-organizing systems as well.

more broadly extended, meaning that we are being more deeply integrated into life. To our everyday minds, however, that experience is very unusual. Descending to the level of the shamanic, for example, we enter a realm that lies outside our culture's reality system.[8]

For the past few years I have met with a group of drummers to explore what the shamanic tradition calls "non-ordinary reality."[9] A meditative journey accompanied only by a steady drumbeat,* non-ordinary reality becomes more like poetry than prose. It has offered me, through imagery, profound insights and growth.

In the group, as we move ever more deeply into the shamanic level of reality, group members begin to experience *shared* images and knowledge. Ordinarily, each member comes with an individual agenda, so the likelihood of generating overlapping or common images is very low. Yet often two, three, four or even more people report having the same images on their separate inner journeys.

The ring of being is extended in all directions. As with the other rings, the shamanic language is related both to the ring above it (in this case, the animal, instinctive), and to the language of its darker half, the dream. According to dream expert Jeremy Taylor, "the shaman becomes the animal in trance and has the animal's experience." He notes, on examining ice age cave paintings, that "in the case of shamanic figures, the animal and human forms are blended into one,"[10] not unlike my dream of the dancing animal-woman.

In discussing the other levels of language, I suggested that the shadowed portion of each ring is less controllable than the lighted

---

* Some shamanic practises use peyote or other mind-altering substances. This one uses only the sound of the drumbeat.

one. The same structure holds true with the shamanic-dream ring. One can choose to explore the depths of the shamanic level of language and while doing so, consciously change direction or end the meditation at will. Most of us, however, do not have the ability to enter, alter or end our dreams consciously.

~

Are dreams real? I think they may be closer to reality than we might want to believe. In our dreams, we participate in a more complex weaving of the dimensions of life. We are given the opportunity to stand both inside and outside our lives, and depending on our ability to remain receptive, we may receive insights about our lives from an entirely new perspective.*

Dreams also provide feedback. Following decisions and behavior changes from the previous day, my dreams have rewarded me for growth with themes of "dancing in the streets," "death and transformation," even "bottomless boxes of gifts." Just as the shamanic experience provided overlap and confirmation of images from others, dreams extend the possibility of feedback even further. In dreams, we interact with self as Other, and with Others known and unknown, living and dead, as parts of ourselves; we commune with other persons, species and realities.

Both shamanic reality and dreams extend the ring of being beyond space and time. Many of us have had dreams which were synchronous, telepathic or pre-cognitive. These experiences, which threaten our conceptions of linear time, are apparently very common events according to both Jeremy Taylor and Eric Jantsch.

---

* The most creative dreamwork I have experienced is the intuitive approach of Richard Moss. He goes far beyond classic interpretation and his intuitive insights are startling.

Dreams are chaotic, perhaps symbolizing more accurately a self and a reality which are neither logical nor consistent. I have heard dreams described as the "language of God, one we are all born with" and as "prayers of the soul."[11] These are descriptions which speak to the mystery and at the same time to something that is an integral part of nature; for, according to Jeremy Taylor, all mammals and marsupials dream. He also suggests "that *all* living things may participate in the dream state…(and) that the phenomenon of dreaming must have an essential evolutionary value."[12] If these statements are true, then the language of dreaming follows the same pattern as the other languages of the model: it is related not only to the rings above it (and image, feelings and instincts have long been recognized as components of the dream), but below it, to intuition and the story of the cosmos.

～

At the level of the intuitive, the separation between inner and outer dissolves. There is no brightly lit section of this fifth ring. All of it is shrouded in shadows. I have no ability to initiate or choose this experience. It comes *to* me, like a gift. It is *all* feedback (though I do not recognize it while it is happening.) The more I trust my intuition to inform my actions, the more frequently I experience synchronicities in my life—another form of feedback.

If we were more skilled at recognizing and interpreting the language of intuition, we would recognize a truer and broader dimension of reality than we do now. Intuition extends the ring of being even further than the shamanic and the dream. My experiences of intuition have occurred most profoundly at the boundary of another's life and death. Under these circumstances, there has been a web of information available, *transcending time and space.* The diary entries which follow are only a few from the week of my

133

first husband's death on October 25, 1968. This series of painful readings extends the ring of being among several people, events, electronic instruments, spontaneous purchases and time:

October 24, 1968. For years I have wanted to start a book of quotations from others' writings that I have found meaningful. Today I bought this soft green leather-bound book with gilt-edged pages. It seems an extravagant sort of notebook for the budget of a faculty wife, but it was very important to me that it be beautiful. (Before I entered the quotations from my collection, I was moved to write three of my own: on love, on marriage and on God. Then I was interrupted and wrote no more.)

October 25, 1968. The *speedometer* on the three-year-old Volvo we got on sabbatical has been broken for weeks, but I feel an imperative to fix it today. I called the local dealer and am very anxious because he says he can't repair it today. I did everything in my power to get him to change his mind. He did not.

October 25, 1968. Milton is flying home tonight at the end of his first national concert tour. I am yearning to see him. Except for one weekend in the middle, he has been gone a month. He's flying into Boston tonight and thence to the Lebanon, N.H. airport nearby. I have friends who are driving to Boston today. It's cloudy and I'm afraid the planes won't fly into Lebanon if the weather's bad. I stand at the phone, wanting to call and ask them to go out to the Boston airport and pick him up. I dial their number four times and hang up repeatedly before it rings each time, thinking it an undue imposition.

October 25, 1968. The plane crashed this night in the mountains ringing Lebanon airport. (After a year of investigation, the FAA decided it was the plane's *altimeter* that was at fault. I had never heard of such an instrument, but I clearly associate it with my concern about the speedometer that day.) We waited for almost six hours to learn if there were any survivors. When I was told that Milton was dead, I looked at my watch. It was 11:50 P.M.

October 26, 1968. On his last weekend at home, Milton had left his briefcase behind. On this day after his death, I looked in it and found a Hallmark card addressed to me. He had often playfully tucked cards under my pillow for me to find in the past. I assumed that this was one he'd forgotten to give me. I opened it. Printed on the front of the card was a clock with the hands set at 11:50. Under it was the message: "I've been waiting for the right time to tell you…" Was the synchronicity expressed in the clock's hands and the hour of Milton's death a meaningless coincidence? Inside the card, the printed message meant to be a joke, was an odd scramble of letters, a nonsense word, a message beyond language. After it, in Milton's hand, "*I really do love you.*"

～●

Right now I feel a bit like Job: "I have been holding forth on matters I cannot understand, on marvels beyond me and my knowledge."[13] This mysterious path into reality leads us down from thinking to feeling, through sensing and instinct, dream and intuition into the story of the cosmos of which each of us is a part. It is a journey of reawakening, each layer more subtle and more informative, rich with the languages of the universe.

On this journey, we redefine what it means to be human. We recognize that we are all indeed receivers and that we are intimately related at every level of being. We discover that we are not masters, but members. In the most humbling sense, we are integral parts of the whole. Only from this position of humility do we discover that our roots are already in place: in our bodies, in the earth and in the ongoing story of life.

Anne Hillman

Then perhaps we can begin to fly as members of the flock.

9

The Tender Connection

When I was a young singer, I practised scales and arpeggios to extend my vocal range. And as I would sing higher and higher, my voice would break from a rich, grounded sound to a high, breathy trill. My voice teacher would shout, "Don't *reach* for it like that! *Don't lift off the breath!* The note's down in your body. *Sit* on it!" But I continued to reach, because, to me, the note was "up" and I never understood her.

I once thought intuition had to be something reached for too. Like my perceptions of the proverbial spiritual experience, I imagined it an ephemeral, almost wispy kind of knowing that floated to some people as if from on high. Such a higher form, while it may be true for some, did not square with my experience. My journey did not raise me up, it brought me down.

Strange, though, like Alice in Wonderland's topsy-turvy world beyond the rabbit hole, what seemed down in my former life, did not seem down now. I felt better for having embraced my worst. What once had been deemed bad, now brought forth something good. In my newer and larger world, notions of good and bad, right and wrong, true or false were far too limited. Those judgments, so vividly portrayed in my dream by concrete buttresses, had bound me in too small a frame. Now I was learning to let my body teach me, and as I slowly opened to its teachings, more of me came alive.

As I began to inhabit my body more deeply, something traced a path down through the spiral of thought, image, feeling and sensation and made them one. It seemed as if there were a fleshly way of apprehending experience, something that no longer happened in my "mind" as I understood mind, something that had no bearing on "reality" as I saw and smelled and touched reality.

I was astonished when I recently looked up the roots of the word "intuition" and found that the origins of the word meant *protection, a guarding. (The birds do not follow a leader; rather, each bird operates independently, following some kind of inner guidance for self protection...)* I believe intuition is a form of protection built into us; that it lies deep underneath our other ways of knowing, not "out there," not "above," but "below" thinking, feeling, sensing, instinct. It is a kind of *knowing at the core* that is available to all of us.

When I experience intuition, I often find myself saying, "It occurred to me..." Sudden ideas arise, as if from outside: new options, thoughts, suggestions, awarenesses. They seem to have nothing to do with *me* as I had always defined myself. They require neither my effort or thought. It is then I realize how severely limited was my previous view of being human. Something in our makeup permits us *to be receivers.* Somehow, we are both smaller and larger than we thought. Quite mysteriously, in the acceptance of our more humbling reality as creatures, not gods, something in us quietly opens up like a flower and listens.

What we hear are the languages of the cosmos; the slender threads that weave us together with all of creation. How do I know this? I don't, in the way we characterize "knowing" in a factual or "provable" sense. Intuition from the perspective of intellect is flimsy. Then how do I know? I *know*.

We have all had instances when we know something, and wonder how we knew. We think of someone far away and seconds later the phone rings and they are at the other end of the line. Or it happens in reverse: the phone rings and an image of the person calling fleetingly enters our mind just before we pick up the receiver. We call it "intuition" and are momentarily amazed, or call it "coincidence" and toss the event aside.

This kind of experience suggests a way of living from a deep place in our bodies. It is not another thing that we can know in our minds and then file away in our storehouse of remembered facts. That kind of knowledge is abstraction. It is disembodied. This is knowledge *of the body*. The body is not an abstraction but a *member*, a member of creation, and therefore intimately connected with all other bodies.

My experience tells me that what we have to this point called "intuition" is something intimately connecting people and life itself in ways far more profound than mere coincidence. Let me give an example:

When I was completing this book, my agent suggested that I really needed an introductory chapter which would provide an overview of what the book was about. As I began to write, all my lofty sentences about meaning and purpose felt very dry to me. I stopped and asked myself—my body—"what do I really want to write about?" Then I waited. Amazingly, I found myself once again at the airport in 1968 awaiting Milton's plane. And so I wrote the pages that begin this book. But then what? How could I connect that event with all I had already written? I sat empty at the keyboard with no idea of how to proceed. Had the day's writing been a total waste of time? After all, Milton had died twenty-two years ago. As fresh as the experience at the airport seemed in the moment of writing, what did it have to do with a book about membership—one among many?

Just then the phone rang. The woman's voice at the other end was unfamiliar. She introduced herself as Ellie, the widow of an architect in town whom I had admired but never met. She explained that he had died just a few months before and that she was preparing to turn over her husband's potential client list to a new architect. She had found our name on an earlier inquiry and wondered if we would we be interested in remaining on the list?

My body was still immersed in the experience of my own loss and instead of answering her question immediately, I replied, "This must be a very difficult time for you…" She began to talk, and I listened to her, knowing from the depths of my being what it was like to confront each day, to feel the loneliness, to go through the drawers and files of a beloved husband's office, making it ready for another person.

"You understand," she said, "you know."

"Yes," I answered, then waited.

She began again with a new urgency. "He's gone. But I'm alive. And it *makes me realize how much I want to live, and to live my life with meaning.*"

140

I was stunned. The coincidence of her call at a time I was writing about Milton had not been lost on me. But this passionate statement was the link I needed for my writing. I had experienced the same urge to live in the months after I was widowed; and the same very powerful desire to live a meaningful life had fueled my labors for ten years, learning how and what I wanted to write. But that passion had become such an integral part of my life that I had forgotten where it had originated. I needed her to remind me at that moment.

She and I became friends after that call. And I was the first to remind her when she thanked me again for listening to her, that it was a mutual need we two met that day.

~

When Milton's mother died several years ago, my daughter and I returned to the east coast and spent several days in the home where the old woman had lived since she was a bride. During that period, we counted sixteen astonishing examples of synchronous events and intuition. I offer two.

This elderly couple had, for decades, tossed pennies into quart jars, and left the jars in closets and drawers. The house was full of them, who knew how many hundreds or even thousands of dollars? We called several banks where they had had their accounts. No bank would take the coins unless they were counted and wrapped. We were already overwhelmed with work to be done in the few days remaining of our stay.

On our last day as we frantically made final arrangements before packing to leave, we made one last attempt. Looking in the yellow pages at the long lists of banks in that city, we selected one at random. I described my dilemma and the woman who answered immediately called me by my first name. She had been a close friend of my mother-in-law's and had just started to work for the bank that week. It being lunch hour, she was covering the phones for the first time. If we would carry the pennies into the bank, she would be glad to count and roll the coins during her breaks over the next few weeks and send us an accounting when she was through.

During the week, we had identified several things to give to my mother-in-law's church. The day before we were to fly home, the minister arrived with a truck to haul away the items, including a washer and drier. While I was upstairs, he attempted to pull the washer away from the wall without realizing it was still connected to the water supply. The valve broke right off the pipe, sending water cascading into the room. The three of us panicked. We had no idea what to do.

Just then the back doorbell rang. There stood a young man who identified himself as a friend of Milton's mother and said, "I just happened to be passing by and wondered if there was anything I could do? I'm a plumber."

At the time of a death, the veil between the reality we know and the larger reality these kinds of events imply, seems to become more transparent. I am not sure that reality is necessarily different at these times. What I recognize, in reflecting on my experience, is that I am so overwhelmed by grief and the fact of death itself, that I am intensely aware of my powerlessness. In addition, the practical demands of such a time are overwhelming. And because I feel so helpless at the combination of these effects, I am more likely than at any other time to yield myself to Life. I open myself in sheer desperation. I *trust* in a way I rarely can under ordinary circumstances; probably because my trust is forged in a doubt so deep. And Life opens to me in return.

When I was learning to turn my life around, one of the most formidable tasks confronting me was to learn this kind of trust. I had spent my earlier life mightily defended. Surrendering those ways of protecting myself did not come easily. One spring week, I had gone away to the shore to be alone and quiet. During my stay, I became aware of a red-tailed hawk circling lazily over the field outside my window. Barely lifting a wing, it glided up on a thermal and then floated, almost motionless, for what seemed hours. Wings spread, it rested on unseen air currents, and played with what came. As the days passed, I came to see the hawk as a reminder to trust.

Something moved me, one afternoon, to step outdoors just as the hawk appeared out over the bluff and circled over the field. I stretched out my arms, lifted them and began to fly along with it. There on the deck, I soared. I banked. I glided up a thermal. I turned lazily, effortlessly. "I am a hawk!" And for that hour of grace, I was.

The following week, I happened to mention this part of my exercise in trust to my therapist, and a strange look came over her face.

"When was that?" she asked.

Because I had written about my experience of "flying" in my journal, I was able to pinpoint the time exactly: "It was a little after 1:00 on Thursday," I replied. I had been a little surprised that she had asked, since in my perception, she was not given to an excess of fancy; rather, she seemed quite reliably conservative. I was more surprised when I heard what she had to say:

"Anne, when I left my office after lunch last Thursday, I was astonished to see a hawk sitting on the ground right beside my car," she gestured out the open window. "When I approached, it flew up in that tree right over there, and sat on the bottom branch watching as I drove away."

A hawk on the ground. In a parking lot. In the city. At exactly the same time I was "soaring." To me, it was the tender connection—the subtle meeting place between psyche and nature.

There is a river flowing underneath my everyday life. It *informs* me if I am aware. It seems to offer suggestion, dimension, depth. If I notice and follow, I am buoyed up, lifted on my way. My story unfolds as if ordered. That is not to say it *is* ordered. I cannot know that. But it seems that way.

Where does the reality I call *real* begin and end? *Can* it be so bounded to the limits of my senses? I already know that the spectrum of colors I see is a far narrower band than exists—that infrared and ultra-violet reach beyond the confines of my "real" world; that my acuity of sight and smell and sound are surpassed by the sensitivities of hawk and wolf and deer.

If my senses cannot encompass reality, shall I permit reason to define a "real world" when my experience already proves it shrunken? Reason, for example, delineates "one" *or* "many." What if we are *both* the one *and* the many?

This is a central question. We have been faced with choices between values, morals and definitions, and we have had to

144

choose a single identity as well—*who we are*. Are we one? Or are we more than that? Might we be simultaneously present to different facets within us? Can we have *both* unity *and* choice in our identity?

Can we be more than we think we are? Can we embrace a sense of self which is inclusive; which accepts a multiplicity within *and without* as self; which does not limit identity to the present tense as we experience it, nor to only the human aspect of creation?

There is a hunger in us for what is real. Jacob Needleman states that we "need a teaching that is understandable to the mind and touches the heart that offers an understanding of the whole of reality."[1] My experience was not one of understanding. It was one of *tenderness*.

This was not tender like Madonna and child. It was raw. Tender was palpable. Like flesh. Tender was utterly unprotected, with the potentiality for being as easily torn as liver. Tender was exposed, thrust out into life like a bag of food hung out over a branch at the campsite with the bears padding below.

No wonder tenderness is a quality unappreciated in our culture. It implies too much weakness and vulnerability to pain, something of the feminine we have tried to erase. But it is what I found under logic, feeling, instinct and intuition. Intuition is a great gift but it is not the same as what I found beneath it.

What I found is not a result of understanding but of surrender. Understanding, for me, was a form of control. Gradually, as I became willing to let go of control—not to know—my intellect released its hold on my feelings. I was flooded with richness, whole octaves of responses to life, sounding joy and grief, gratitude and rage. When I sang, I no longer lifted off the breath. I brought the highest notes out of the depths of my body. Feeling an aliveness that was almost unbearable, I imagined my cells expanding to contain the fullness. New feelings of terror and humiliation appeared, then slowly moved aside to reveal my humanity. My dreams were peopled with beasts and birds of prey and in them, as I prowled the forest floors and soared the skies, I came to respect the powerful instincts within my body.

Each experience of increasing depth demanded a yielding. Trust. As a result, something new started to weave itself in my cells. That something is what I call the tender connection. The tender connection is not intuition. Intuition is a faculty that perhaps dances at its edge. The tender connection with the unity of all things is like a threshold. There we experience an elusive sensitivity that seems more like an embedded natural wisdom than our more isolated, fragmented logic. Receptive to this language which our body knows, even if our intellect doesn't, *we are both more autonomous and more integrated within creation—because we are more fully ourselves.*

The tender connection is our true identity. I don't believe that it can be taught. It is *bought back.* There is a price we pay to redeem our fundamental and exquisitely vulnerable human core. It is a costly redemption.

This tender connection is our very *being.* It is the subtle meeting place between psyche and nature. Inhabiting the body at this depth is living at the quick, a vulnerable and creative threshold where we become intimately present to the life around us. Undefended, our deepest selves exposed, we participate in a *ring of being.* We are like a note tuned to a chord. We *are* the chord.

This quality of communion between our inmost selves and our surroundings gradually weaves in us a new and inclusive identity. The more we tune to our core, the more our boundaries widen and melt. We begin to see ourselves in others and others in ourselves. We let go our hold on what we think we know and tremble as the energy of the unknown rises within us. We stumble on the lair of a wild creature in our bowels. Our kinship with the grasses and hills grows. The beasts of the forest and soaring birds of prey acknowledge their counterpart in us. The whole world enters as if through our pores and an exquisite thread of vitality spins itself across chasms of separateness.

～

This, the universe, is our body. Intuitively, we know this to be true. Mystics have echoed it. It is at the tender connection that the boundaries of space and time dissolve and we experience the seamless communion of self and other, past and future. There we discover, as if running our fingers over a Moebius strip, that what we thought was inside or outside is really one single surface. One story.

10

The Cosmic Story

Today, through our telescopes, light, billions of years old is coming into view for the first time in human history. With our newest technology, we are able to see and celebrate the twenty-billion-year unfolding of the universe in our own time. In that very real sense we are present to the early creativity of the universe. It is that creativity, to which we are now heir and servant, on which our entire lives and the life of the earth itself depends.

The universe *is story*. As we become more able to read it in starlight and fossils, embryos and genes, we may modify its details slightly; and as the story becomes clearer, its importance to us does also. The story of the universe, unlike our local myths and religious traditions, is the only story which all human beings share in common. It is the foundation for our functioning as an entire species. All of us are called by this sacred story of the cosmos in which we have our home. We, as its very young creatures, shall tell it to our children thus: [1]

149

Listen to me, and I shall tell you a story which began long, long ago, and is still going on in you. It is a great drama which you have been born into, and you are here to contribute to its unfolding. It is your story and your children's story and your children's children's story.

Out of the deeps there exploded, some twenty billion years ago, the origins of all that is, spewing fire and power and light, a blazing beginning that we have come to call the Fireball. Out of that mighty event has burst everything that was ever made or known—every star and every child; every painting, every grief. Granite and trees and compassion and awe; hawks and deer and thoughts and love. All were born of that first passionate mystery, the first creativity of the universe which is still pouring forth.

Billowing out of the Fireball came galaxies whirling into being over millions of years, like snowstorms of stars. Out of that first moment came galaxies. Came all the protons and neutrons which make up the universe. Came flowers, birds, your body. You are the Fireball: all the particles, the energy in you, were created out of it. Your body is made of starstuff. It is a mystery...

Five billion years ago our earth was formed and all the planets which surround us. We can watch it happening before our eyes: look up at the night sky! Look at the numinous light from the deeps of the dark, timeless past. Our beginnings, an ongoing mystery—now!

Eon after eon, the creativity unfolds: always a surprise. Never a moment repeated. Never another person like you. Never another galaxy like Andromeda. Every snowflake a unique event. Every single event shines with its own luminous beauty. Each flower. Each stone. You.

All that you are was fashioned by the stars, the planets, the plants and animals which came before you. All were required for this moment: all of the beauty and violence; all of the joy and pain of evolving; all of the sufferings which led to creation. How shall we celebrate all of the beauty and the terror that has come before us?

Our Story is a work of art—a single unfurling event. All of the universe depends on each being in it. Each depends on the whole. Mountains, rivers, lizards, children. Each of us is necessary. All of us belong.

We are all on a journey together. The most important journey of your life is the journey to the center of the universe. It is deep. It is here, unfurling itself within you and about you. The fireball was the first center. But now, look deep: Into yourself. Into another. For at the center of each created thing, the real spills out—reality, creativity and power. It is to a center which is everywhere that is the holy journey, and there are many who will teach you along the way: people and animals, plants and events; the desert will teach you, and the mountains. Strangers. Your heart. Perhaps your greatest teacher will be your own tears.

First you need only look: notice and honor the radiance of everything about you. Be glad for the being that cries out of all things to be seen. Play in this universe. Tend all these shining things around you: the smallest plant, the creatures and objects in your care. Be gentle and nurture. Listen. We are all learning to listen with all of our selves: Our hearts. Our bodies. And that which hopes in all of us: our very souls. Once we listen, then we can respond. Once we see, our response can be only joy.

Who would not be joyful? Long after it was first formed, the earth's center gradually began to create, as centers do. Under the pressure of gravity and nuclear forces, it heated up and brought forth its metals of every kind. Molten rock, laced with veins of silver and gold, copper and lead, platinum and iron, flowed beneath the crust of the earth. All the bubbling in the depths raised up the mountains in all their glory. It created the seething volcanos, and out of their fuming gases and vapors, the salty oceans were formed.

Did you know that there was only one time in the Story that oceans could have been formed? Only once in the unfolding mystery of the eons were the conditions ready for the coming of oceans. They can never be created again. That is true for everything we know: the time of creating life out of no life is over. Our human intelligence has been formed once and for all. There was only one moment in all of history for you. *And for your own creativity.*

Millions of years passed and very slowly, deep under the oceans, tiny bacteria began to fill the sea! Over a long period of time, these living beings began to eat up all their food until it seemed there might be nothing left for their lives. Would life end right then and there, when it had hardly begun? Then, when it seemed most hopeless, the creativity of the universe took a new step. Out of the great masses of bacteria continuing to survive in the old ways, a few found a way to live on sunlight. And as these autotrophs took in that light energy and used it to sustain themselves, they created the single most important chapter in our creation story since the Fireball itself. Without them, the coming of the prokaryotes and, later, the single celled plants which created chlorophyll, none of us would exist: neither the later animals which needed oxygen and ate the plants; nor we humans who depend on both plants and animals for our sustenance.

We are children of light. All of us, we and the other creatures on earth, live on the light from the Fireball. It is light present in our own sun—light which plants transform into energy for their own growth. Light which was first transformed by creatures that could not see. (Yet when we open our eyes, it is almost with their exact process that we capture light.) Sunlight. And so we are brothers to the grasses, sisters to the apple tree, children to all the animals who came before us: the snake and the dinosaur, the wolf and the hawk, the mosquito and the tortoise. We are relations. Countless species of plants and animals weaving together a design, slowly and carefully over millions of years—all in passionate relationship to the sun. 3500 million years since life's fragile beginnings in the ooze; what care it has taken for life to nurture and sustain its millions of forms and expressions over the eons!

Look! Now we can see it! Creatures appearing over a thousand million years, displaying an explosion of creativity in the fossil layers of our earth: sea creatures to trilobites to dinosaurs. Algae to ferns to redwoods. All have been there waiting for us to finally see the story as it has unfolded. We see it under microscopes, through our telescopes, in the Grand Canyon and in fetal development. In every display of its facets and creativity, the universe is telling us to look! Join in! Care.

Celebrate! Can you imagine what it was like when the flowers finally came to earth, bringing ravishing beauty and brilliant colors where there had been none before? Bringing stored energy for the first time in nut and fruit and seed, so that creatures didn't have to spend all day feeding to survive? Can you imagine the kind of celebrations we humans might all create together, to honor—instead of wars or generals or a local religion—the coming of flowers and their meaning for life forms as diverse as bees and squirrels and people?

Celebrate! How might we celebrate the coming of human beings? What a moment in the story! Could we enact what it felt like to emerge in an animal body—and be the first to look around in wonder at what we saw? And then to begin to express that awe in painting and dance and song?

At first, we knew no difference between ourselves and all the rest. We saw the trees and the animals, the lightning and the sunshine as ourselves. We lived in ecstatic relationship with these beings; looked up at the starry night sky and felt "delirious with bliss."* They were our companions. They spoke to us. For four million years we lived together, participants in the wonder, wandering from place to place, carrying what we needed on our backs, hunting and gathering our food in the wild. *We were wild.*

Then, ten thousand years ago some of us learned to farm; to grow our food and tend our animals so that we could live in one place. Life was easier for us. We became domesticated. And everything changed. From living in small tribes of 25-40 people, we began to grow communities of thousands. We began to lose our feeling for our ways and our relatives in the wild—the animals and the forests became more distant cousins in our hearts. We lost our wildness forever. Our innocence and our ecstasy.

Because our mothers and our grandmothers in those days worked the land, they guided our communities. Their particular skills of relatedness and sensitivity to the others of the earth community were sustained by a perception of the earth as loving mother, the provider of abundance. Our ancient grandmothers owned the land and passed it on to their daughters. It was a long period of peaceful living. We shared what we had among us. And

---

* Quoted from a Wodaabe man, member of a Stone Age, nomadic tribe, in Werner Herzog's documentary film, *Herdsmen of the Sun*, Interama, Inc., 1991.

because we didn't accumulate things at first, we did not resent each other.

Just like the stars and the earth and the creatures before them, so our ancient grandmothers' and grandfathers' creativity flourished: They made pottery and baskets. They wove cloth and craft. They sang songs and told stories to one another. And out of these stories and songs emerged the great early myths; the symbols, heroes and heroines to express the meaning of their lives: a whole framework for our human spirit and for our relatedness to the earth. To the universe.

We can still see one part of this chapter of our story in Crete, where the abundance of the earth is painted on ancient walls and vases; where joy and graceful play between men and women are honored as they endlessly tumble in brilliant colors over the backs of painted bulls at the palace of Minos.

In the meantime, while some of our early parents and grandparents flourished in communities, others of us kept moving with the animal herds and developed different strengths. When our nomadic mothers were bearing and caring for children, they needed to depend on the strength of our nomadic forefathers to protect them. Because we faced different kinds of dangers and harsher climates, it was important for our fathers and grandfathers to be brave and strong warriors. These tribes wandered all over the face of the earth. They traversed every continent. And then the Days of Cold began. Those ancient grandparents sought the warmth and eventually found the great river settlements that were our other heritage. (If we look at that region today, we can still see with the eyes of nomads the astonishing beauty and grace of Egyptian women carrying water as it has been done for millennia along the river Nile. We can still feel the unresolved pain and

struggle of our tribal ancestors in the desert lands of the Middle
East.)

Then came the drastic change in the unfolding of our story; a
major break in our two ways of life.* For in the coming together of
wanderers and farmers these two lines of our human family
clashed. Because of the loamy richness of the soil and the warmth
of the sun, the earth provided those of us who lived in the river
valleys an increasing abundance. We began to build storehouses
for our goods and to keep our surplus in large vats and urns. And
as those of us who were tribal suffered the dangers of the great
Cold Days of our history when the winter never ended, we became
aware of the great store of food and goods in the villages. We were
hungry and tired from the journey. We wondered at the wealth
before us and wanted it for ourselves. We conquered the gentle
ones who had not learned to defend themselves. And we decided
to stay.

With the cold winds at our backs many more of us came from
distant journeys and discovered the riches of the villages. Those of
us who stayed had to learn to protect the land from those who
would seize the harvest. As more of us came together for safety in
numbers, we created cities and built high walls around us. We had
to learn a way of organized warfare, for the nurturing ways of our
mothers and grandmothers of the farmlands no longer protected
us.

---

* This part of the Story has yet to be refined. There are currently two opinions of how these
civilizations blended. The second, and less accepted at this time, is as follows: As farming
families increased, their children spread out in search of land to cultivate, intermarried
with the hunter-gatherers, carrying language and agricultural techniques with them. This
theory is based on a scattergram of genetic patterns across Europe studied by Dr. Robert R.
Sokal, Dr. Neal L. Ogden and Chester Wilson of the State University of New York at
Stonybrook, published in *Nature*, spring, 1991.

Out of this need for strength and for power came something new: dominance. The idea of winning in battle soon spread to extending power in other domains of life. The powerful ones of us began to dominate everyone else: some of us were categorized as part of powerful groups, others of weak ones; men gained complete power over women; the people who owned the land had power over those who worked it. In using other human beings in this way, we had enslaved ourselves. Even the earth came to be seen as something to be owned, dominated and controlled.

Out of this moment in our story came more great advances in our thinking processes and in our civilizations. At the same time, it was a period of great losses. It was the moment in our story which is at the root of our current ecological, social and personal pain.[2]

Out of the mighty clash of these cultures, out of the idea of domination and control were forged a subject/object consciousness such as we have today. No longer were we one among many, participants in wonder and related to the earth community. We developed a separate sense of self. We each became an "I." A subject. We began to see each other and the rest of creation and the universe as "other." Objects. As a result, we were freed to think in a whole new way. Abstract thinking came into being: philosophy and astronomy, mathematics and geometry all burst upon the scene.

And politics. For out of the same conflict, the idea of the state arose.* In this period, our communities grew to 100,000 people,

---

* I differentiate between "state" and "nation" thanks to an article by Bernard Nietschmann in *Cultural Survival Quarterly*, September, 1987. "Nations are geographically bounded territories of a common people...on the basis of common ancestry, history, society, institutions, language, territory and (often) religion. Nation peoples clearly distinguish themselves from other people(s)...A state is a centralized political system that is recognized by other states
(footnote continued at the bottom of next page).

and we began to develop organizations to control people and
goods. Rulers and priests, warriors and merchants became the elite
ones of us: a few with a great deal of power who ruled the many.
Today we call this use of power "hierarchy," and it has come to be
a model for our entire modern world: for our families, our religious
institutions, schools, corporations, governments, international
economies and political relations. It is also the model for our
minds. In western civilization, we prize intellectual and ego control—at great cost to the fulness of our beings, and the richness of
our relations.

Like our ancestors who developed a separate sense of self, each
of our great states, the great Classical Civilizations, experienced
itself as an "I" and sought control. As states, we began exploring
the whole world, in the hope of acquiring the riches of other
regions. Gradually, trading our accumulated goods around the
world became more important to us than farming. Soon violence
and competition for turf, for wealth and for power surrounded us.
We have lived in that condition ever since.

When we lived in the forests, we knew our experience in
nature to be sacred: the stars, the stone people, the four-leggeds,
the wingeds, those that crawl, the sun and all that was. When we
lived in our communal farming villages, we knew the earth and
her abundant provisions to be sacred. Those of us in the herding

---

(footnote continued from the bottom of previous page).

and that uses a civilian and military bureaucracy to enforce one set of institutions, laws and
sometimes language and religion within its claimed boundaries...regardless of the presence
of nations within its boundaries that may have preexisting and different laws and
institutions...A nation-state is a rarity today...Nations without a state make up (the) Fourth
World of internationally unrecognized nations...(These) encompass most of the world's
nations, about a third of the world's population...The present global war is fought largely
by the Third World...Out of 120 conflicts, 98% are in the Third World, and 75% are
between Third World states and Fourth World nations. The Third World War is a conflict
over territory, not ideology. Territorial autonomy for nations would end most wars."

tribes brought a new kind of worship which has also been with us ever since. Five thousand years ago the story of the creator God emerged: reflecting its culture, this was a masculine god, a transcendent god with concern for and power over the people. Compared to the more concrete realities of previous sacred experiences, this kind of god was an abstraction. A sky god.* Gradually, as the story of the new God evolved and was interpreted, the sacredness of the earth and all of creation was lost. The sacredness of being was lost to us. And the ecstasy of being alive.

Each of these major changes in our human ways of living has occurred more rapidly than the one before. When our ancestors emerged out of our pre-human beginnings, the time we lived in the wild spanned hundreds of thousands of years. When we became settled and farmed the warm river valleys, we think it lasted about 4,000 years. The rise of the great states took place in a few hundred years and lasted about 4,000 years, until 1800.

The most recent change in our human ways has taken less than 200 years; and it has brought devastation to the earth. The Industrial Revolution, the creativity of our own grandparents and parents, has led us to the present dilemma in our story. This age of industry, made possible by the theories of Bacon, DesCartes and Newton, exploded in a burst of invention beginning in the 1700's. Electricity was snared from the sky. Black coal, dug from the earth, fired new furnaces to power textile mills. Then steam and smoke began to belch from ships on the sea and iron horses on the land—the locomotives. Oil, sucked out of the ground, powered Model T Fords. Huge dams stemmed our rivers and factories lined

---

* These statements do not deny the reality of That which we choose to name "God" with our words. They refer to how we *define* (and so doing, *limit*) the limitless nature of That-which-has-no-name. Indeed, this entire book celebrates that Mystery.

159

the shores of our rivers and lakes. Chemistry and medical technology exploded.

Our dilemma is a two-edged sword. Petrochemicals strewn on the earth increased by an order of magnitude the bushels of corn and wheat our farmlands produced—and poisoned our land, the waters, and many creatures which fed there. The exclusive use of hybrid plants reduced the genetic pool of available seeds. Medicine saved and healed countless lives, with unexpected consequences. And finally, with nuclear technology, we discovered both a new source of power and a weapon of mass destruction.

The inventiveness of the last two hundred years has brought us health, immeasurable wealth and freedom. But it has also completely changed the face of the earth. Unwittingly, our creativity has made us destroyers; the technology meant to free us has so run away with itself, we do not seem to know how to stop it. We have tamed electricity and nature, juxtaposed incredible modes of healing and overpopulation, landed on the moon and created mass starvation. *Precisely because of the intelligence we prize,* we live on the brink of the extinction of all life.

We know this place. The story I have been telling you is a story of the creativity of the universe. We have been here before. About to starve, the autotrophs learned to feast on light. Facing extinction in the Days of Cold, our wandering ancestors learned to cultivate their food. Time and again, faced with annihilation, life has adapted. Once again, we must learn wholly new ways or perish.

Each of us needs to participate in this unfolding of the story. Each is a center of the creativity of the universe itself. More than any other time in history, we are called to offer our own deepest creativity at a time of great crisis. We are called to journey to the center of the universe. Our intellectual creativity is too limited. So are our emotional and instinctual responses. We must find a way to weave those together into new ways by tuning to something more profound. Something our intellects cannot fathom or contain. For it is only at the center of each being that what is truly real exists. And when anything displays its innate nature—what or who it really is—that is where the universe itself is able to create with care.

The story I have been telling you is a story of care. Over billions of years, life has sustained and cared for an ever growing display of its beauty: a sheer beauty of being. This beauty is a manifestation of variety and differences that we have just begun to see. The story of care is one of nurturing that variety and honoring differences.

As we begin to make the descent down the other side of life's mountain, we learn to rely less exclusively on our intellect and our determination. As we become more willing to admit that we do not know, we learn to trust. As we increase our trust, our masks fall away, and we are able to see more clearly our real human natures. As we realize more of who we really are, we discover we have been making the holy journey to the center of the universe. Then, as we experience and accept all that we really are—within as without—we grow in care. We begin to embrace others *as* ourselves, and learn to live as one among many.

The story of the universe is a story of hope. It calls us out of our despair to become all that we are: each of us fully human, relating and functioning as a whole species, as integral members of the earth community, in a leap of loving such as we have never imagined. This is our hope.

The entire universe, the entire story up to now, was required for you and me to stand here today. All the creativity of the Fireball, of the supernova, the stars, all the genius of the plants and animals and peoples before us were needed for this moment. All these things in the universe call to us to be seen, to be felt deeply within us, to be known. We need to reach out to embrace them, and to recognize that in our cells and our genes, deep in our souls, they are. We need to feel in the longings of our hearts, in the callings which attract us, they are. We need to re-member all that has gone before us, from the Fireball and the stardust to the ferns and the redwoods, from our earliest human parents in the savannah to our present grandparents and parents—to know we really do carry them in *who we are*. We need to stretch out our arms wide to the universe and say: ***"THIS IS OUR BODY."***

Part Four

~

A Capacity to Care

11

Three Cosmic Births

Who will come to the feast in which the self is consumed? Who will accept the invitation to become tender enough to experience the beauty and the majesty of the universe? The famous? The successful? I think it will be those who have always come. The failures. The poor in spirit. The broken. The grief stricken.

The grief did not begin for me until I was tender enough. Then it seeped through my tissues, rolled like the interminable waves of the sea and sank into the soft sand of my shores. Something new grew in that damp clay. Was it my very soul? I don't know. But something emerged in me that loved beauty. That knew both caring and joy. A mystic perhaps, and one that wrote poetry I didn't understand.

~❧

Grieving the oldest love,
      that lost gold in the heart,
      a shining
      entrusted to the deeps.

All connectedness has lain
      a sleeping princess
      behind the great wall
      under the lilac bushes
      scattering royal purple
      melting in the raindrops
      mingling with the grief
            of the universe.
Life:

      will you reveal yourself
      only
            in this brokenness?[1]

~❧

A poem has its own life. It rises when it wants, comes from a
place of its own. Midway through the writing of this one, something from the mythic depths took over and began to boom. You
can feel it in the images—the wall, the lilacs, the royal purple—
but more in the mysterious rhythms which intoned, for me, some
more distant memory. A memory of a great rocking like the immense rolling of waves against a shore.

But I had no idea what this poem meant. How to explore it?
Since, during the preceding two years, I had practised with the

drumming group how to learn by following a meditative drumbeat, I decided to "journey." A method suggested by shamanic practises in other cultures, it might lead to a different way of understanding what the poem had offered me.

I put on a tape, lay down and closed my eyes. The insistent rhythm of the drum soon led me deep into an inner world which shamanic teachers call another reality. I find it a place which illuminates the everyday experience *we* call "reality."

...resting on a steady drumbeat, I journey deep into the shamanic imagination of the human race. I find myself riding on a hawk's back, soaring far out over the ocean. From a hawk's eye view, the sight of the shoreline mingles in my heart with pictures of womb and tears. What a strange association...

I did not understand. Several days later, the images began to reveal themselves:

Ocean, womb and tears.

Three salt seas.

Three places of birth.

What the deep world had offered me were three evolutionary images of birth.

The first birth: We are born out of the ocean, all of us creatures. We are bonded to her, our common mother. Our tears, our blood, our sweat still taste of sea salt. When our ancestors the fishes crawled up onto land, what a lonely and terrifying journey! Was our new environment hostile? Were there creatures which would endanger our lives? How should we defend ourselves in this new habitat? Our old defenses had been pushed to their limits in the sea or we would not have taken such an incredible risk. We were surely, as we are now, *driven to transformation*.

The second birth: Each one of our human births is the second birth. We emerge from our mothers' wombs, like fish who've become mammals. Indeed, a whole journey similar to the evolutionary journey of animal life takes place in that interior sea where we are formed. Still, we are begun and born human beings. And we are born helpless.

And so we come to *the third birth*, the birth of tears. Life calls each of our lives into question, at one time or another. If we choose to answer that call, rather than to ignore it, we make the slow turn back, facing the way we have come and the person we have become. After the dream of the one-way sign, I began to travel "the way back" on the road of my own life. I questioned everything. In the course of this exceedingly difficult commitment, I challenged my assumptions, my beliefs and my self image. The layers of my history and my self gradually peeled away in the search for truth. I grieved the false sense of strength that willpower and control had offered me up to that point. I grieved old beliefs that had given me meaning; truths and roles and things known; the safety and comfort of an identity that no longer served me. I grieved those I loved as I released them: friends, parents, children, husband. And I grieved my hopes and dreams. They were the hardest of all.

Subsequently, my old picture of my self began to fall away. As I mourned the self-sufficient, confident, in-charge identity which had buttressed me for decades, I came up against a void inside me. It felt like I had no self.

~

There is a dark hollow
where all my dreams were.

Now the terrible soft feelings ascend
as I grieve
each shining hope,
each perfect companion,
towering construction
and seeming certainty.

Yes, they were make-believe;
but held me fast
until I could bear to see.[2]

~

It was a moment of extreme vulnerability. I had no familiar
place to turn. And so I turned to the emptiness inside and asked.

Out of that silence in me came a yearning. It seemed almost
ancient—one that went beyond my personal history. Now I would
call it a yearning for the Mystery. At the time, the best expression
I could give it was a yearning for depth.

A question occurred to me: might the "way back" imply a
longer road than just my own lifetime? I experimented. I began to
re-*member*; to connect back imaginatively, first to my forebears,
then to my kin among all humans; then back through the unfurling of the rest of creation. I explored the three evolutionary births
at depth, and discovered that it was like picking up lost stitches in
a garment full of runs.

It was indeed a re-membering: For I discovered that my own personal decisions and losses were, in many cases, the same as the decisions and losses of human history. In seeing my own story as a small version of the story of humanity, my identity was knit up and rewoven into the rest of creation.

I think this imaginative journey back is an important one for all of us. I believe we all have a longing for depth: a depth of truth, of meaning, of relationship, of purpose. Our culture's demands require us to live on the surface much of the time. I am coming to view the need for depth not as just a personal need, but a social one as well.

There is something reciprocal between our human past and our cultural preoccupation with the superficial. It has to do with what happened in our human history. I am suggesting that our very survival, as individuals and as a culture, may depend on our journeys back. Through these journeys we might learn once again to coalesce, as organisms have tended to do since the beginning of time, in order to function as a species. For it is at depth that we are linked with other individuals, with society and with the earth.

With the creative.

And with life.

As we connect back through the cosmic story, some of our memories of loss may be of actual deaths. Others may be more broad, such as the loss of childhood. Still others may be larger scale losses of social transformations, such as the loss of a community or a farm. The journey back is filled with cosmic events. Each event represents a leave-taking of what we have known and cared for. It is a cumulative process of *grief*:

❧

I remembered the women leaving infants in daycare, wanting to be with them and at the same time wanting to grow professionally.

I remembered the huge armies of refugees on every continent, leaving a whole way of life, suffering the loss of their countries in search of sustenance and hope.

I felt the loss of making ritual together; the celebration of our human story. Of how we forgot to be poets and singers and tellers of tales, and let the Famous Ones entertain us instead. I remembered how the children stopped singing and painting in school. How the culture acted to dismiss each loss for the "greater good." How it promoted shallower forms of what was lost: educational toys for genuine play, T.V. for theater, cocktail parties for community.

I remembered my father swallowing hard, his jawline tight as the industries he worked for transferred him to one city after another for the good of the company. I remembered my mother and her friends weeping before each of these ruptures in their communities. I remembered how our fathers became strangers in our lives, who got off a train at six o'clock and left in the morning before we were up.

I remembered the stories of my great grandfather Hurlbut who simply could not make the transition from the farm to an office in the late nineteenth century. He considered himself a failure. I remembered what those men who left their farmlands gave up in those days: a deep relationship with the land, an attunement with the natural rhythms of sun and season, a capacity to directly sustain and support their families; an integrated membership in community and with the earth. Abundance.

I felt the pressing back of tears, the gritting of teeth, tightening of jaw, the hard swallow, as we collectively left parts of ourselves behind in order to progress in life. I remembered each event leaving its mark on our souls and bodies. Each was a *holding on* of pain. Each holding on was passed to the next generation, in psyche and in body. And I knew from my own experience that *the price of letting go was feeling that pain.*

I saw us at the foot of a great waterfall of tears; each generation bearing the losses of those who had gone before; each carrying a heavier burden of grief in its bodies. As I remembered, I felt the losses at each great transformation in human history.

I tumbled back in memory, back to the period of our neolithic settlements. I remembered how we came to value strength and power because we needed to defend our settlements from invading tribes. I remembered how "being like a woman," came to be shamed. How some of us lost our tenderness. How men and boys learned to control tears and feelings.

Now women in organizational settings struggle to do the same things.

I felt the sheer physical effort it has taken to control our tears in order to meet these cultural advances. How we bought our new selves with social, physical and emotional control. How our muscles, organs, ligaments and cells have paid the price. I recognized in my own body how I had hardened, tightened up, lost feeling and receptivity.

I continued to remember, further back in history, as we left the tribal-shamanic period for life in those small agricultural communities, how we lost our membership in the forests and savannah. How we lost what it felt like to be a part of the community of nature. So doing, we lost the direct guide of our instincts for actions; our sense of smell, our ability to sense the location of prey or threat. We left, and left the majesty of our wildness behind; we left our selves as part of the animal kingdom. We lost certain freedoms along with certain dangers. We lost our animal sensibilities.

Our primal bodies.

Our primordial souls.

Our savage fury. Our vulnerability to life. Our awareness. Our ecstasy.

Perhaps the greatest loss was our experience of belonging to the mystery of the universe.

This was the primal time, the time celebrated by the story of the garden of Eden. As I remembered that garden story, I felt again that loss of instinct as I moved instead toward knowing. Toward choice.

In eating the fruit of the tree of knowledge of good and evil, we had begun to learn to decide...*to kill a part of.* In learning to decide between forest and settlement, we had to kill a part of something. Each time our human story changed, we lost something else along with the forest, the matrilinear settlement, the classical culture.

Each time, we killed a part of ourselves.

173

We need to reclaim who we are. That is why we need the third birth. It is a birth out of tears for the severing of old bonds and for the loss of our selves, our souls and bodies. A birth out of intense grief *into an unbreakable bond with the universe, an immediate experience of connectedness with all being; a birth into care*.

I experience this relatedness throughout my entire being. It is neither a thought nor an insight nor a sentimentalization. It takes place in body, mind and heart at once. They are no longer split. It is a state in which I *behold* the beauty of all the universe—as if I were in love with each unique expression of its creativity, *center to center*.

This is not mere nature loving or the appreciation of things that are pretty. First and foremost it is *wonder*: I am stunned! Why should there be anything spinning out here in space at all? Something in me delights in each particular and unique thing it beholds. As it is. The beauty of a granite rock, a luminous planet or a crusty iguana in its naked presence. Our bodies and souls sense— *are*—this beauty of presence when we ourselves are inwardly naked. *The real beholds the real*.

We have all experienced moments of this kind when we know ourselves to be one with the core of life itself. This relatedness is our human expression of the bondedness in all of the universe— between moon and tides, between sun and earth, between every being and the stars.[3] In every expression of itself, it is the longing of the earth to be known.

There is a promise of this bonding at the time of each of our three births, for each birth creates a living bond. But the deeper integration begins to take place during the birth of tears. Now, thanks to the images of wisdom imparted from the shamanic depths, my poem's meaning became clearer to me.

174

For the birth of tears is a birth into care. Care, *Kara,* is the an-cient word for grief. When I search more deeply among the roots of the word anger, I find it in the Icelandic, *Angr.* That word also means *grief.* Care brings with it the knife-edge of anger and sorrow. The four are inseparably bonded. Care. Anger. Sorrow. Grief.

Split apart, as our distinctions tend to do, the truth of who we are is lost to most of us. The ancients spoke a more complete truth when they created language. Today's more splintered definitions *deny our species's deepest wounds.* Nor do those definitions reflect the combined passion and rage that sustained us when we were wild in the garden. *Could we all but weep, our weapons would lie rusting in the deeps. Could we all embrace the fierceness gifted us by the universe, we might begin to care.*

~

...The hawk and I continue to hover almost motionless above the coast. Before this flight I had seen the meeting of land and sea as a meeting of opposites: Land. Sea. Two separates. I remember what these opposites have symbolized to me in the past decade—male and female, form and possibility, certainty and ambiguity. How I have struggled with polarities! Now, as we hang suspended in the pale sky, I remember the dream of the compass without a needle, given me at the shoreline. The compass was to show me a new way of getting my bearings. I had understood it to mean that I needed a centeredness in order to thread my way between the opposites. That understanding has served me well. But my view, until this flight with the hawk, had been from the ground.

Now I am older. The view has changed. The hawk's view is broader. The curve of the horizon includes land and sea—no longer opposites, but part of one entity—Earth.

If we are to care, we need to let go the boundaries of our self definitions and include more of who we are. Some feminists, for example, tend to ascribe the human quality of caring to women because they are nurturers by definition.[4] I think that when I make these kinds of distinctions I am not flying with the hawk, but am still earthbound. My experience tells me that the quality of caring I am describing comes as much out of the dark and male dimensions of my being as the more visible nurturing, feminine one; that it is also born of deeply felt anger, destructiveness and grief. This birth of caring is the product of many opposites, including its own. It is a "oneing"[5] of the opposites.

Each birth is a "oneing," a healing, but we can't see that clearly until the third birth. When we experience the third birth, it is as if we were riding a hawk's back. We not only see the inclusive curve of the horizon, we also see that life as it evolved onto the land became a oneing of the land and the sea. *That new life itself is the bond*. It cannot be split apart into "land" or "sea." It is whole: a new creation.

Each of the three births is also the birth of a new creation out of opposites. In the first, as we have seen, a new breathing, ambulatory creature is born of the land and the sea.

In the second, a child, a new being is born of male and female. Then, so briefly whole, each child soon begins to create two kinds of reality. To *decide*. We learn to decide from our cultures and our parents. From one parent, many of us learned to honor strength and intellect; from the other, feeling and relationship—first in family, then among friends and community. We men and women have borne these two apparent opposites like the land and the sea on our separate ways for countless generations. We have not understood that just as the horizon joined earth and ocean, something joined our two paths.

176

Right now the whole earth is in the midst of the journey between these two opposites, male and female. Every person engaging with issues of sexuality and of partnership is engaging in a cosmic issue, not merely a personal one; for the decisions we make as a species need to include the creativity and the values of *both* sexes. It is a dance that has great meaning for all creatures, indeed for all creation. It is crucial that we sense its import in the whole picture.

The new creation of the third birth is care. In care—compassion—the polarities between self and other, between joy and pain, can no longer be separated. The birth of tears creates a living bond between all dimensions of being: we remember the other in ourselves, recognize ourselves in the other. It verifies the vital connection not only between male and female but between persons of all colors and walks of life. We experience our kinship with the creatures of the forests, with the earth itself, the sea, the sky and the rivers.

The prior bond, *the glue* between earth and sun, *was the creation of life itself* in which both earth and sun are fused, indissoluble. The bond between man and woman is also a new creation—a *child*. The new creation of genuine relationship is *care*, born of joy, anger and grief.

The new creation within the individual, then, is a most creative act: *Who one is*. One's whole self. Undivided. Body, mind, heart, soul...and more. Norman O. Brown offers the idea of "heads as seeds." *Seeds!* What a beginning!

~●

In myself, an acute longing to be *known* has accompanied these births. I don't mean fame or public recognition, but rather *to stand revealed*. Transparent. I discovered that it was also a longing to give expression, so that what I created might enter the universe, a gift, a *naked saying*.

We each have a creative gift. Part of the damage our specialized and professionalized culture has done is to diminish our belief in our own creativity. Some people's very lives are a creative act. Some people listen. Others sew. Some teach. Some invent. Some try something new in their own relationship. Some plant flowers. Some endure. Each is an offering, a work of art, a new form.

Right now, this book is my creation. It is likewise a "oneing" of opposites. In its form and content and voice, I have tried to respond to Gregory Bateson's last question: "What is the interface, the *glue* between logic and metaphor?"[6] I had supposed we would ultimately discover love to be the bond between the two. But now I think that the question sets up the wrong kind of search. Rather, I believe that love as we know it is the *process* between polarities, but the *bond is the new creation, the new thing, the new form as the expression of that love*. That unity cannot be broken into parts.

This is why the cosmic story calls us to make the journey to the center of the universe, the center of creativity and power. Our deepest creativity is needed now, *a creativity woven of all that we are*. It is in that painstaking journey to our own centers, as we peel back and accept layer after layer of our humanity, that we find ourselves naked. At that center, the real spills out. There, the center and circumference of the compass dissolve endlessly into one another. It is the center which is everywhere.

Undefended at our core, as we were at each of the three births, we discover ourselves beloved. There the universe can create through us with care—care for *all* of its radiant display. Then, perhaps, we of the human species, open to a love we do not know, cannot define or comprehend, will also discover ourselves to be one in the unfolding cosmic event. In that actual *experience* of our intercommunion with all of the earth community, we might tap the wisdom we need to guide us over the crucial years ahead on this planet.

This chapter began with grief and tenderness. Tender, I saw for a moment the terrible beauty of what was real. I felt both the terror and the awe. I grieved then, and sang songs of praise. The gift of the dream compass had given me my first bearing. But the view from the hawk's back gave me a deeper one: the bearing of life itself—as it is.

Caring—compassion—born of grief and praise, heals judgment, binds wounds, celebrates differences, accepts all possibilities. It offers a yes to all of life.

12

Integrity: The New Ecological Identity

Human beings are part of the whole, called by us the 'Universe,' a part limited in time and space. We experience ourselves, our thoughts and feelings as something separated from the rest—a kind of optical delusion of our consciousness. This delusion is a kind of prison for us, restricting us to our personal desires and to affection for a few persons nearest to us. Our task must be to free ourselves from this prison by widening our circle of compassion to embrace all living creatures and the whole of nature in its beauty. Nobody is able to achieve this completely, but the striving for such an achievement is in itself a part of the liberation and a foundation for inner security.

—Albert Einstein[1]

181

When I was four or five, sitting in my backyard sandbox, I became aware of a profound sense of loneliness. That is where I first remember the hollow sensation in the pit of my stomach and the tight dryness in my throat that accompanied it. I was often in the sandbox alone. Its edges were splintery and warm and the sand left on them from the night before would stick to me and scrape my thighs as I shifted position, squatting there in the morning sun. Sometimes I traced the grain in the sunbleached wood with my fingernail as I listened to the high whine of my mother's Electrolux inside the house. Or I would dig my toes in the sand and notice how white and crusty it was on top; and underneath how its grey dampness still smelled of salt from Jones Beach.

I remember just sitting there. Sitting and waiting for something to ease the loneliness. Patting and packing damp castles into pails and paper cups. Wishing them peopled with fairies and princes, all cascading with magical stars. Feeling the emptiness in the middle of me, an emptiness that continued into my adulthood, playing on underneath my days and nights, like a slow, solemn *basso ostinato*.

The presence of people did not fill it.

Two years after Milton died, I brought the hollowness home to my apartment one night:

~

I have spent my morning at a circus,
sound-blaring
eye-popping
people-full hours of red purple yellow

popcorn cotton candy hay and barn smell
sounds blaring, pitch assaulting.

My child with his head in my lap asks
"Is it over yet?"
People swarming, bumping, laughing:
No-one touching.

I have spent my evening at a cocktail
party,
Black satin and flowered silk,
Chanel and Arpège
dill spread and cheese puffs,
people smiling
brilliantly chattering:
No-one talking. . .[2]

❧

I sought relief from that separateness in countless ways: in intellectual pursuits and projects of all types; in social activities, in relationships. I sought it in churches, in jobs, in marriage. Relief was only temporary, if at all. Somewhere, I had lost my way.

I am not alone in these experiences. Sophie, a friend, laughed wryly as she remembered shortly before she died, something her sister had told her: "You know, Sophie, I think you were born without instructions." I have seen a pervasive alienation and a deep longing for community in my culture. I see it in organizations where I have worked. In the young. In the elderly. In the desperate search of single persons. In marriages.

The artist tells us about ourselves. I saw a man's hand in a painting that expressed this same anguish. It is a painting of a couple totally without relationship. They are seated close together yet their eyes are haunted because of the real distance between them. They neither see nor know one other. The man's hand is enlarged with vastly elongated fingers, as if they might magically extend across the gulf between them.*

The poet speaks to the same issue: John Donne wrote, *"'Tis all in pieces, all coherence gone."* These artists are addressing not only a personal and social context, but a larger question—living together on an earth where there is so much suffering. How have we become so disconnected? I think it is because we "lost our instructions" early in life. We lost access to the languages and wisdom buried deep within us.

I believe that there is hope of a reciprocal relatedness between our souls and nature; of a communion with the stars and the tides, the earth, our selves and one another. If we were able to reclaim our human heritage, to *feel* and *experience* our relatedness to others who are different from ourselves, to *know in our bodies* the human bond we share across boundaries of nation and race, culture and religion, would that not make a difference? Might we then be able to feel the consequences of our decisions and actions more empathically? If we were able to *experience* and *sense* our connectedness with all the earth community, or let our *intuition* of it guide us more deeply, would we be able to make more compassionate choices at every level of our lives?

This has been the nature of my quest: following a tenuous thread from the disconnection and loneliness of the sandbox so that the feeling of separateness might be healed; leaving the surer

---

* Oskar Kokoshka, *Tietze Couple.*

footing of culture's expectations for the unknown; trusting new forms of guidance; starting over. The thread has taken me along many unexpected paths, and often unwanted twists and turns. Yet it was in the unwanted nature of those turns that the thread which had become unravelled began to reweave reality in a new way.

Acceptance is central to this completing process of the self. Integrity begins with an increasing willingness to *accept the nature of our humanity*, to attend the living creation of which we are a small part, and to learn from it constantly. Integrity is the *what*, acceptance the *how*. Integrity is the fabric, acceptance the thread which binds it. Acceptance creates whole cloth from separate strands, heals splits caused by the nature of language, judgment and fear. Acceptance provides the missing, inclusive balance to our culture's emphasis on *knowing*: on definition, analysis, problem-solving, improving, trying. It weaves together *what is*.

The process of acceptance has been the hardest thing I have attempted. It required first of all that I accept myself. Could I indeed say yes to this half-finished creature caught somewhere between heart and groin? I had always assumed that the statement "love yourself" was a blanket statement and a blanket act, as if there were a light switch to be activated somewhere and self-acceptance would happen of itself. In my life that did not occur. Instead, I addressed one facet after another of myself that I found unacceptable. Slowly the nature of my humanity became apparent to me. Gradually I could let myself see dimensions of one behavior at a time in many different circumstances, begin to acknowledge it and see how it was affecting my life. But try as I might, I could not make it go away.

One of the most difficult of my attributes was that of control. It had been suggested to me in my twenties that this was an issue for me. I had struggled with it for almost three decades to no avail. One winter day my husband was driving us across the wide Sacramento valley toward the Sierra for a weekend in the snow. I sat in the passenger seat, very quiet, stunned by a sudden realization of the enormity of my need for control.

In despair, I must have decided to meditate, or at least quiet myself down. The time passed in silence. Suddenly, a question struck my awareness like lightning : *"Could you accept your control?"* I was astonished. Hot tears spilled over as this new voice that I did not know spoke from some other place in my consciousness. It did not sound like the harsh judging voices which had accompanied me all my life, but had a gentle and caring tone. Half embarrassed, I took its counsel, put my arms around myself and rocked me back and forth like a baby, there in the front seat. It was the first moment of compassion for myself that I had ever known.

This was the creative moment, the beginning of love. Like the ancient fishes before they crawled up onto the land in a desperate search for survival, I had done all I knew how. For almost thirty years I had been trying to erase or push away this single aspect of myself. In the despair of the void, the new way was born. *Receive. Accept.* These were not tears of self pity but of gratitude, and perhaps the beginning of some humility. This is how I was. Perhaps I could let me be human after all.

Acceptance was a slow process. As it grew, I found I had compassion for other aspects of myself, as well. Some I have described: the witch, the weak one, the tender and vulnerable child, the griever of losses, the beast. There are many others. Attribute by attribute, I opened my arms wide and took myself in. Each time, I wept.

"Gather your strength and listen; the whole heart of
humanity is a single outcry. Lean against your breast to
hear it; someone is struggling and shouting within you...
The heart unites whatever the mind separates, pushes
on beyond the arena of necessity and transmutes the
struggle into love... What is meant by happiness? To
live every unhappiness. What is meant by light? To gaze
with undimmed eyes on all darkness... Out of an ocean
of nothingness, with fearful struggle, the work of
humankind rises slowly like a small island." [3]

Is this how god is born in us, bit by bit, as we weep for who we
are, that we are merely human? As we scoop ourselves back up in
loving arms? As we weep for others—so like us—and gather them
up too?

I do not know how god is born. I do know that as my self-
acceptance grew, I found a new dignity. I did not need to "do," to
prove my value by achievement. For I was standing on something
solid inside myself instead of trying to balance on the edges of my
being where the mask hid me from others. I was standing on a
different ground. I could be who I was, not who I thought I ought
to be. This was the place of tender connection—the truth at my
own interior. Now I *could* be known because my acceptance had
begun to make me transparent.

Accept everything. That is all. [4]

Acceptance of the seemingly unacceptable is what brought the
deer. I embraced myself and acceptance healed.

There is a prior embrace in which we are all held, the starry curve of space in the universe. I have come to recognize the following statements *as its laws:*

> By the very fact of our birth, *we are*
> *each chosen.*
> By the very fact of our birth, *we are*
> *valued.*
> *We belong.*
> *We are related.*
> *We are beloved.*

High in the Sierra one night, I lay alone in my tent and realized that relationship in a new way.

~●

KIN[5]

Here on the ground
all of creation sleeps

trusting
we are held
and breathe starlight

coyote
I
deer
refugee
forest child
homeless one

188

> without walls
> we share
> one bed

～

No longer a stranger to my true self, I was increasingly my original, created and tender human creature—one among many. It was then that a communion began to spring up between me and those who surrounded me. I felt a reciprocity between me and other created selves and creatures. This was the intimacy that I had sought. Fully disclosed, I saw that we were all woven of the same cloth.

We are earth stuff, a geological formation. Handfuls of magma and mud given form over time. Built on the vertebrae of fishes, fired by the rituals of serpents, standing on the shoulders of mice. Deep with the dimension of thought, we are loved by life, nurtured with all that is needed.

～

> Sometimes in the late afternoon, I see the wild, dry meadow grasses afire with sunlight against a backdrop of darkening hills. As I look at the fragile stalks silhouetted there, I feel a catch in my throat, almost as if I were in love. It is more than just an appreciation of nature's beauty: we are in dialog, the grass and I. Acknowledging something. Connected. More than merely providing breath for one another, we are part and parcel of the same *stuff*.
>
> *"Hello,"* I whisper, in recognition.[6]

189

❧

Rilke said it beautifully:

"...their newest convert, who is now like one of them,
all those silent companions in the wind of the mead-
ows."[7]

This capacity for communion is the foundation for what I call
an ecological identity. As we become more aware of the untamed
and unknown within us, we begin to claim the pulse of the wilderness within ourselves as well. The sap in us begins to flow. The
shuttle moves more rapidly, in an opposite mode from control. It
weaves the presence of other persons—particularly those we think
are different—into our awareness and identity. It teaches us to
celebrate those differences. Into our fabric it weaves strands of
creatures and air and soil and water that are also part of ourselves.
We identify with plants and trees, with shared DNA, with life
itself which pours through us in our brief moment. We begin to
care, not because of righteous indignation, but because all this *is
who we are*.

❧

As our identity expands, we discover we are both one member
of the chorus *and an expression of the song which is singing us:*

> I awoke before dawn in Ecuador, in a leaf-covered
> hut on stilts near the Napo River, a tributary of the
> Amazon. Creeping outside the tiny building, I
> clutched the thick bamboo railing tightly as I made
> my way along a slippery wooden catwalk to the end
> of the clearing. Raised several feet off the ground

above flood level, it swayed slightly under my weight until it ended abruptly at the edge of the dense rainforest. It was absolutely still in the steamy darkness. I sat and waited.

Before the first light I heard a faint fluttering in the wet canopy above me. An unseen bird started to sing. Then the locusts began their slow rasping on the forest floor. Louder and more insistent they grew as the parrots joined them. The monkeys commenced to quarrel overhead, and songbirds added melody to the growing awakening. Tick, tick, tick, another unidentifiable entry at ground level caught my attention; then I saw overhead at least fifty vultures in a tree. Waiting. The volume grew along with the light. In the distance the screaming roar of a howler monkey cut through the din.

Perhaps, somewhere in that rainforest, some humans sang or danced their aliveness in the sunrise. My body wanted to participate in that magnificent chorus celebrating the light! It was like a tapestry of stories being told.[8]

~

Integrity is *not* a model, not the toddler's toy, frozen into form. That is only an attempt to tease out different colored threads, to sort out experience. Integrity is *story*, with no beginning and no end. *Integrity is the eternally new creation, spontaneous and increasingly diverse—a tapestry of the interwoven stories of all beings as they*

191

~~behold one another.~~ Here, amidst diversity and rooted in change is
where the creativity and the dynamism lie—ours and the great
creativity of the universe.

To have an ecological identity is to accept oneself as story, part
of this continuous interweaving of one's own and the larger story
of life. That gives the kind of perspective that welled up in me at
12,000 feet in the Sierra:

At the tree line
the granite ledges swell,
heave up, rough, to the sun's warmth,
undulate naked in the light -

then cleaved
by winter's icy chisel,
rupture along hidden meridians,
crack open
to expose a glistening heart
as massive wedges fall away
under an eon's hand.

I lie small in my gray cloth tent
surrounded by the debris of that giant attraction—
eternal, erotic dance between earth and sun,
so much greater than my timid palpitations—
and listen within
to all the rest tumbling down into time,
sharpening these ghostly precipices
arching, sensuous in the summer heat,

then falling,

falling

in the night.[9]

～

Looking back to the dream on the mountain road which called me to turn around, I can see that it was *a call to intimacy with life.* The first requirement of that relationship was an ability to be on intimate terms with all that I was myself; for intimacy requires mutual self-revelation. At the time of the dream, I hadn't the slightest idea what there was of me to reveal! There was much work to be done, for I had lost my way long before that moment of profound loneliness in my sandbox. That alienation was the result of socialization. As a child of the modern world, I had learned to decide and to control, gained the use of words, and lost the sense of things. I had indeed lost my instructions.

In the long run, however, it has been a journey out of a personal history to find my place in the natural order restored; a release from preoccupation with myself as an individual, into a membership in the life fabric.

～

In this search for identity, we have been chronicling what has been lost at a personal and human level, as well as that which has been never found. As we weave our own stories into the tapestry of life around us, we begin to develop a wholly different perception of what it means to be human.

This larger identity is *formed in a group.* It cannot be formed in isolated nuclear families, as our first identity was.[10] We need the

combined energy and wisdom of larger numbers. *"So many are
required for the truth!"*[11] Perhaps this is the strong pull to community and group life that many of us feel in these last decades of the
twentieth century. Perhaps a new archetype of the group is coming
into being.

That archetype requires Integrity. Integrity implies an integration of soul, heart, mind and body. It is not only an addition of the
feminine mode. It is an increase in the human repertoire of
thought; an increase in the collective consciousness. It is humanity becoming all that we are, being made *a new thing.* A luminous
thread in a seamless garment. A song. Integrity implies a *new way
of being*—with others and in the universe. It implies caring: a
quality of attention which involves a total commitment to looking, listening, feeling, sensing, intuiting, being. This resonance is a
presence that may become a kind of "knowing together,"
(con-sciousness.) Might then some higher intelligence begin to
move our species *as a group,* so that each of us becomes an instrument, attuned to the whole flock?

We are describing the human *being,* literally *homo essens.** To
be a human being is to be one's own essential self. To be *essence.*

I am that I am.[12]

Our history to date has been the history of *homo sapiens*, "man
who knows." Knowing has brought us great treasures at the same
time we have done great damage with it. We have not yet become
human *beings* at a cultural level.[†]

---

* I have coined a Latin word here since the ancient Latin language reflected a human
history in which "being" was not a recognized state. Therefore the verb *esse,* "to be" included no present participle.
† While consulting to industry, I coined another Latin phrase, *homo laborans,* to describe
(footnote continued at the bottom of the next page.)

Thomas Berry states that we humans must be recreated at the species level. He says we need an intimate relationship with nature and with the earth. Surely we have become estranged: living in tightly packed urban and suburban settings; breathing recirculated air in high-rise buildings; shielded from the wide arc of the sky by roofs over our heads at home and work, in cars, trains and planes. With electric lights to extend the day, how can we know the night? With schools and jobs and appointments run by the clock, how can we know the rhythms of nature? In this world of specialization, we long for integration. There is the call of the entire created community resonating in our souls. Where can we begin to do the necessary work to prepare ourselves for *the new thing?*

Intimacy with nature requires our *presence.* We need to be present to our bodies—to be attentive to *our* nature. And we need to be present to what is happening around us: to look, to really see, to listen. Nature, in our culture, has been relegated to a backdrop for our activities. We can find new ways each day to give it our attention.

One of the great gifts a mother gives her young child is to adapt herself to her child's natural rhythms—hunger and sleep, activity and rest, closeness and exploration. One of the great gifts we can give ourselves is that same rhythmic intimacy. We can learn to adapt not to the clock, but to our own needs for food, rest, sleep, solitude.

(footnote continued from the bottom of the previous page.)

the Industrial Revolution's product: "working man." That situation continues to deteriorate. A study for the Economic Policy Institute by Juliet Schor of Harvard and Laura Leete-Guy of Case Western Reserve confirms that the average American worker put in about 140 hours more work per year in 1989 than in 1969. In addition, paid time off (vacation, sick leave, holidays and personal time), fell 15% in the 1980's to 16.1 days per year, compared to European workers' vacations of *at least five weeks*.

I have moved—left the business world and learned to grow vegetables. I have come to live where the deer are; to let a single day be ordered by the sun's and moon's journey across the sky, the tide's rise and fall; to celebrate the sun's illumination of the meadow as dawn sweeps across the grasses; to sing its kindling of the sky at dusk. I have practised synchronizing breath with the rolling of the waves; begun welcoming quiet in my own life with the coming of darkness. At times there is an expectancy in me, and a brief sense of the presence of wild creatures all around me gently opens my focus for a moment, like the petals of the sea anemone.

This quality of presence contributes to intimacy with all of our kin. *We can give no greater gift to another than the quality of our attention.*[13] Integrity has to do with mutual presence. This is a quality of attention from center to center. From what is to what is. Full attention to another calls for a quieting within, a simple satisfaction with the moment. An acceptance that *this is what life has put before me right now: this person, this task, this experience.*

Deep calls to deep at the sound of thy cataracts.[14]

Perhaps Integrity can also be translated: real calls to real. Integrity requires an increasing willingness to attune to the nature of the reality of which we are a part and to act on its behalf. To care in the simplest of ways: to listen, to plant seed, to tend, to provide water or food or shelter for other persons or creatures. To preserve habitat. This is the paradoxical state of letting go and being responsible. *"Tend your garden,"* said Thoreau. But what is my garden? Who is my brother? My sister? *Who is* my neighbor? The earth in all its exuberance is our community now.

~

I am more than I thought. *I am bread.*

~

Integrity is not something we do, nor can we make it happen. Integrity is something we *are*. It is lived in the languages of embrace and letting go, the language of the waves, the seasons, of breath and of human love.

Can we envision ourselves as a radiant tapestry of intersecting realities? Interior life and outer experience, creatures and cosmos, logic, imagination, mystery? Perhaps this is the new creation: the embrace of an identity which integrates person and universe so that they reflect one another, a reciprocal evolution, an unsplit god.

13

Hymn to the Mystery

If Integrity is the figure, then Mystery is its ground, the infinite unknown, a depth brimming with the constant creativity of the universe.

When I was young, I lived by a wild mountain brook that cut through a deep gorge rent by some great prehistoric sheet of ice. The brook was a presence. The roar of its rapids never ceased.

Our home was a small inn in Vermont. I remember leaving it one afternoon when the sultry August air hung heavy. My chores were done. Heading across the fresh-cut grass to the edge of the gorge, I descended the granite steps until the way became too steep, then picked my way backwards down a long ladder. As my feet touched the uneven bank, I could feel the washed river pebbles through the soles of my sneakers and my breath eased. I was in my secret place.

There was my rock. Granite, it dominated the others and sparkled in the sun. Shoved above the rapids by the forces of many floods, it looked like a long narrow dais, smoothed by years of water wear. I squinted and it seemed to be floating on pillows of foam.

I made my way across the stepping stones, shedding the other world with every step. With a final leap, I landed on the rock and stretched out full length. The granite was warm and hard. Its head end was tilted up slightly, letting me see the water droplets tossed into the air and caught by the sun like fractured diamonds. As I looked through my eyelashes at the colors, I let a hand trail in the water and idly wondered what the old mill had looked like when it stood on the far side of the bridge. Nothing but rubble there now.

After a while, I slid off the rock, scraping my thigh, and felt the sting as the cold water hit it. Wading upstream, I held my own against the white water beating at my stomach and legs. Then, working my way to the spot where the water was shallow enough to sit, I turned away from the sun and leaned back against the current. Licked by the fast water, I sat on the polished stones at the bottom of the river, looking far into the darkness of the gorge as it bent out of sight.

My world.

High above me was a different world. At the inn, my parents were preparing the evening meal. Waitresses were setting the tables. Guests played croquet on the lawn; others sat rocking on the porch. On the far side of the concrete bridge high overhead, I could see the top of the faded red clapboards on Mr. Thomas' general store. He was probably cranking the polished handle of the cash register for the last time that day. There was still the evening milking to do at his barn. Cars rushed in both directions across the bridge but I could not hear them. They were soundless behind the roar of the water which swirled around me.

In delight I leapt, splashed on my belly, felt the smart and flashed downstream, a glistening trout. Clambering onto my rock to dry, I lay face down, cheek on hand, watching. The busy world above was obliterated. Here below, was my world: dark, wet, roaring, hanging with tangled roots and damp moss, smelling of mud and green.

The world above was a place of answers. My father had them. So did my mother. The teachers in school had them. Books had them. But here on my rock I experienced life *in a different way.* Here, I wondered.

⮮

I wonder still. And when I do, I am in that world-beneath-the-world again, as it was in the brook. The smells, the breezes, my feelings, sensations, creative ideas, all are present. I am focused *and* diffuse. On my rock, while I was acutely aware of scrapes and cold and light and cars above, I was at the same time more woven into the total fabric of life in the gorge: animal, mineral, vegetable. Wondering, I was one among many.

Those two worlds—the brook and the world overhead—form a template for much of my experience. For a long time I was part of the striving world-above, reaching for greater skills and knowledge, trying to do what was right, wanting to excel. Even as I lived it, it seemed like an uphill journey. Intuitively, however, I felt that what I was looking for lay, like the life of the gorge, *at depth.*

It was the beginning of a different way. Some sense began to form in me of *increasingly complete* dimensions of life, dimensions that existed beneath the surface. There was something at the center to be tapped. Deeper than intellect and feeling; deeper than sensing and the breadth of the intuitive; deeper than the story of life itself. What...? Was it just my imagination? How would I find out?

As it happened, it was something I had neither the power to search for nor to solve. Instead, I had to become lost. In finally accepting that I was lost, I found my doorway to life. Then life itself became my teacher and taught me in its own way. Called by a dream to journey back down a twisting mountain road, I began mining my days and nights for what was real. Each turn of the downward spiral became a reawakening to a deeper level of self, requiring greater and greater honesty. Each turn rewarded me with the embrace of a larger identity.

I had to *learn how to learn* from life. As I learned to follow its increasingly subtle clues, the thread in the tapestry which had become unravelled led me toward the depth of being itself, toward mystery.

The paradox of the mystery is something like the image of the pyramid of rings. Mystery lies all about it, and at the same time, fills its core. The dream compass at Point Lobos expresses both these dimensions: circumference and center. So too, are the story of the universe and our own individual stories part of the same paradox: At the depth of the universe lies the mystery. *At the core of our identity lies mystery.*

> You are not only a piece of the unfolding. You are the
> unfolding; and you are the silence that is present behind
> the unfolding.[1]

It is to that silence, to the mystery at the core of life, to a
center which I cannot locate, that I attend. I attend it in the
stillness and in the darkness. *Is it love,* I ask? *Is it the creative? Is it
the energy? The life force? Is it wisdom?* Always, I am called, *Go
deeper.* The mystery is not love; it lies beyond love. The mystery is
not wisdom; it lies beneath wisdom. The mystery is neither the
energy nor the creative. *Go deeper.*

A wise person once said to me that there were three questions
which all human beings repeatedly ask of life: *Who am I? What is
god? And what am I to do?* The deeper I have looked, the more
these have depended on one another. How can I have any sense of
what god means for me, unless I have a sense of myself? And how
do I make meaningful choices about my life, without having
examined the first two questions? The more I have asked, the
more they have become one question; and the more unanswerable.

They are fathomless.

We yearn to live sacred lives. To align ourselves with meaning.
To consecrate our actions. To sing to the stars our assent. To live
sacred lives at this moment in history requires something more
than religion, psychotherapy, political action or community-
building. *To live sacred lives requires that we live at the edge of what
we do not know.*

This is the different way. The plight of our lives and our world is
the result of what we know. Hardest for us to hold is an attitude of
not knowing. At every step of the journey, I have had to *unlearn*
what I had been taught, in order to learn something more true

from life. Ideas and beliefs, moral attitudes and values, almost everything I had thought to be true was repeatedly turned upside down, like the wonderland Alice discovered beneath the rabbit hole. Learning how to learn from life was learning not to know. I remember Jim, a wise, black man, reminding me to "be teachable." It was one of the most important learnings of my life.

Stephen Mitchell calls it "Sabbath mind."[2] Richard Moss suggests the same state when he asks us to give one-seventh of our attention to *that which we do not know*. It is then we attend the mystery. It is then that we may be receptive to the new thing, to that which is dancing at the edge of our souls.

There are as many levels of this phenomenon as there are languages of the cosmos. The gifts of the unknown are subtle. They are like hushed suggestions or hints. They manifest in a new awareness: an entirely new feeling, or a fresh sensing of the reality of the moment; an intuitive interpretation of another person's need; a deep trust in the mystery to give shape to one's days.

~∙

I have had days when I could enter *not knowing* moment by moment, as if I were entering the movie of my life one frame at a time.

~∙

I remember taking a walk with that intent. One step. Into a new frame. One breath. Let go of the last frame. Step. New moment. Step. New moment. The world lit up. I discovered everything fresh. All categories and labels dissolved. I saw every tree, smelled every fragrance as if for the first time. Each bush, each bird, a new thing.

For some reason that day, I turned and looked behind me—and was transfixed by what I saw. A poem wrote itself in the moment as I watched the beauty swirling around my head:

∼

Unknowing, I enter
each moment
—a doorway—
and passing through,
find I am trailing butterflies. [3]

∼

The butterflies were like an unexpected gift, a symbol, an emblem of the soul. They have always symbolized a rebirth for me. But that day, they seemed to confirm a way of being: a beauty in fragility, in resting lightly in the moment, the same way they themselves rested on air.

When I enter each moment as a new creation, I am living at the quick. It is a place of great vulnerability, a creative threshold. I cannot always live in that state—it is too difficult—but when I do, all things are made new. There is a quality of joy in this continuous loss of my adult-in-control self. It leaves room for the mystery to…what…? *I do not know.* I only know that when I give my attention to *that which I do not know*, it is not on myself. And in that moment, everything is sacred. And very simple.

The motorcycle journey was an experience of the different way. I did not know where we were going nor did I know the way; in letting go my boundaries, my plans and mental frameworks, I discovered I had opened myself to the unknown and was flooded with life. In an instant I lived in an entirely new context—a relationship to all of creation—and found myself questioning the basis for my own human identity. After that adventure, I saw the relationship between the many-layered experience of that one day and the events of the decade which followed. This was a context that went beyond space and time.

When the context changes, everything changes. I remember waking my husband, George, in the pitch dark one October morning, calling him to come out into the field and watch the full moon in the western sky. As it slid down the back of a Monterey pine in the middle of the field, the sun began to rise behind us and turn the sky a deep red. We stood stock-still in our bathrobes and watched that great star, our earth and its moon hang in stupendous balance. In that equilibrium the frantic rush of commuters on the distant freeway was lost in the immensity of time. And we two humans standing in a pasture were forever changed. We no longer saw ourselves poised at the center of this vast rising and setting. Instead we faced toward the west where the moon was slipping past the horizon, and saw reality. We were not still while all moved about us. With the deep red eastern sky behind us, we could feel ourselves falling—falling forever backward with the earth into the eternal sunrise.

~

It is this shift of context from self to something larger than self that is ultimately important. This is where we get our bearings for the different way. Nature provides us with an expression of the mystery. But mystery itself lies beneath nature. Giving attention to that mystery, remaining in a state of not knowing, is a *way of being* in the universe. This way of being creates an opportunity for us to be receivers; to create permeable boundaries in our individuality. Then we have our bearings centered on what is real.

If we are to live lives of meaning, lives which are truly responsive to the plight of the world in which we find ourselves, we need to consecrate them to something more than the activity of "the world above," the world of action. We need to attend what is real. To nurture the capacity to stop. To be still. To listen. To begin in our bodies and feel. To follow the curve of the spiral shell down through layers of ever deepening truth, until we can no longer understand—just be in awe.

We need to learn from the seamless garment of creation; to listen to the languages of the cosmos—a communion of love. What is the language of a scalloped-edged butterfly floating on the wind? What is a mountain's? What is the language of a four-hundred year old oak tree that stands in my garden? What is a star's?

What is the call of our human family? The call of life?

When we begin to listen for this language of communion, we discover that our identity is forever changed. We realize that we are already exploring the different way. When we'd thought we were lost, we had only lost that which defined us as separate selves. In losing those roles and dreams and beliefs, we found the doorway to our real selves and to a new human identity. Now we are going beyond our individuality.

Right now, in these times of upheaval, the sense of the human family is emerging in us. In the same way, we are becoming aware of our membership in the community of all life. Within these rings of being, we are each developing an awareness of our identity as one among many. There are many of us on this long journey home. And there have been many before us.

Our first task has been to begin to learn new ways of being ourselves. My friend Ann says, from the vantage point of her 76 years, "Integrity is being real." First, increasing numbers of the human family began the hard work of accepting ourselves as we are. Then we dared to show that self to others. We began to become transparent.

As we became more authentic, we discovered we had already begun to learn new ways of being part of a couple or a friendship. Until recent years, our intimate relationships had been less diffi-cult because they were shaped by roles and expectations—behav-iors that were *defined* by our culture, rather that *informed* by our souls—by who we were. These definitions were part of our *know-ing*. They kept us more in control of ourselves, tended to reduce conflict, maintained certain balances of power. Rather than encouraging an increase of creativity and love, they confined us to acting out parts scripted by others. Worse, they kept us from being ourselves in any full sense of the word.

The newer ways of being in relationship have meant that both partners have dared to reduce the powerful reins of control on themselves and to be seen for who they are. The risk is surely greater, but so are the rewards: for herein lies the possibility that we may love and be loved for ourselves.

At the same time we reduce the control on ourselves, we are releasing our control on the other. These ways of honesty and of letting go tax our relationships to the core, yet profoundly enrich them. For we are given the opportunity to live lives that are real and open to the emerging creativity of the universe.

Simultaneously we have been learning new ways of being part of a group. Instead of relying on the authority of leaders or codes of beliefs to hold us together, we have been exploring ways of membership that honor differences, confront categorization, explore collaboration and trust. The ways themselves are varied: experiments in community, groups that explore their process, twelve step programs, therapy groups, groups which meet for prayer and meditation.

They all invite an opening into what is real. They all call us to be honest and to be our essential selves. These groups are not easy to inhabit. In them, we discover a basic truth: *We cannot change others. We can only change ourselves.* We learn that becoming real requires exceedingly difficult and painful inner work. Invariably, that work requires our attention to a context larger than our own egos.

We become real in relation to what is ultimately real. As that relationship deepens, we come to know the experiences of *communion* and of *presence*. Just as the wild iris spoke to me in its own language of presence when I became receptive, so too does the greater reality. We all know moments like these—moments in which we have felt one with others and with life itself.

When I was a musician, I sang great choral works such as Bach's B Minor Mass, Beethoven's Ninth and Mahler's Eighth Symphonies with the Boston Symphony Orchestra. Our chorus rehearsed each work alone for many months. Yet in the final rehearsals and performances with the orchestra there was a newness to the experience, a passionate, ongoing interpretation and creativity. We were vibrant with wonder, as if we embodied a living question. Alert in a new way, we were each finely attuned to the possibilities of the moment, a nuance of intonation, a heightening of phrase, a new subtlety of expression. As we listened to our collective creation in the actual process of being created, this quality of attention provided an aliveness and a freshness of performance that had not existed before, no matter how hard we had tried.

This aliveness was never so great as under the conductor, Leonard Bernstein. The man was a lover. Each of us responded to his conducting as if we were his *only* lover, at the same time we were one among many. We sang as one chorus, yet were individually responsive and responding. But our real inspiration was not this person who stood on the podium. The man himself was awed. Our inspiration—and his—that to which we were attuned, was the presence of *the music*, and at the same time, *each other*—*all* of us: singers, conductor, instrumentalists and audience, *in communion*, attuned moment by moment to the whole, to the power of the music pouring through us.

Attuned to that which informed all of us, and to each other, we were a larger intelligence. Led by our hearts we were soaring with the birds. Each one of us, singing alone, yet in concert, expressing something given, yet improvising at the same time; focused on the beauty of the music, hearing our own voice, yet listening and blending note by note with other voices, other parts, the soloists, the strings. It required the exquisite attention of our entire bodies, our hearts and minds and souls. Our senses, our breath, our celebration.

*To live lives as passionate—lives that are sacred—depends on the quality of our attention. We attend to the infinite and to each other.**

---

* Richard Moss on numerous occasions has discussed the two great commandments and has asked *what does it mean to* "Love God with all your heart and soul and mind and your neighbor as yourself?" There are great similarities between these thoughts and many of the spiritual practises of both east and west.

These are not two, but one law. To support this level of attention requires our full presence—our bodies, instincts, hearts and minds. We must *know ourselves to bear the mystery*.

I have been in groups which give their most profound attention to the silence of the mystery, and to each other. In those groups of two or more, I have felt the sheer *physical* power of the mystery on my body, directly and immediately. There have been times when it was as palpable as the forces pressing on me in a jet takeoff. I have felt enveloped in density. I have been magnetized, held fast. I have been infused by tangible space, bathed in an unfathomable current. Stunned by light.

If there were smell, I would call it perfumed. If there were taste, I would say it was sweet. If there were quality, I would call it gentle. If there were form, I would call it voluptuous. But there were none of these. Only the power of something unnameable.

On this experience of the group energetic I stand. It is an experience of *resonance*. A hint of flying with the flock. Oriented to something entirely new, something I cannot conceive, I am for a timeless moment embedded. Embedded, I am myself and I am *am not.** My identity is surrendered—or replaced. I am neither the one nor the many. My entire experience of relationship is shifted to a different plane. It is like a bond. I experience it as sacred.

Identity, intelligence, attention are no longer *mine*. I am part of the dance. I am the dance itself.

The sacred bond comes into being by letting go—in surrender to the mystery. But the mystery which we attend remains unknown.

---

* This repetition of words is intentional.

❧

Thus, the first two questions—*Who am I?* and *What is god?*—end in darkness. The third—*what am I to do?*—is equally uncertain. Still, if I am alive, I must act. And if I want to *live* my life, then I must choose.

How, then, shall I live? With my own life, I want to serve the mystery. But how shall I discover what that choice consists of? Robert Frost suggested taking the road less traveled by. That is what I call the different way. The core of that way is surrender. *All I really have to surrender is my own experience.* I have nothing to offer but this moment: this awareness, the sensations, the urges, the fears, the goals. Everything. Whatever is happening right now.[4] I can surrender my knowing. Let go my grasp on life. For what? To tune to *that which I do not know.* To be open to what is evolving through the great Being of humanity and of life, so that the unknown may become embodied. To give every bit of my story to the unfolding story of life and to its creativity.

Can I embrace the unknown in each moment? Welcome life on life's terms? It is hard for me to be unwilled. Harder still to become undone again and again. Yet it is gradually becoming a way of life in the service of life.

Living at the apex of the pyramid of rings, we humans cling to our knowing. We think we have the power. We think it is the way to hold on to love. Yet I have been told that *the only power I really have is to let go.* This loss of control deepens with each turn of the spiral on the journey down. At each turn more energy is released. *Letting go is the transformation process.* It is a process that makes a home for the mystery.

212

The act of love is the surrender of self into life *as it is*.[5] This is a love larger than our word "love" can contain or express. It embraces all of life and does not judge: tragedy and war, suffering and joy, creativity and destruction. Beauty. Death. The Other. Within this embrace of life as it is, lie acceptance, forgiveness, healing.

When we let go enough into the depths of our being, we are in communion with all of creation. We are center and circumference. One and many. Self and other. Without difference. We are receivers of one another. Then the mystery which surrounds and informs us is served. At depth, we discover that our aloneness and our bondedness are one. Ours is an identity with all beings. Herein lies our healing, the end of loneliness.

Like the two spheres that were one, spinning in opposite directions, I cannot hold that reality in my thoughts. To stay grounded, I have had to find other ways to honor the paradox of our human identity. I have discovered that it is in the simplest, most minute experiences that I can begin to do that. Then I am at home, my created self. I belong. Walking. Looking at a tree. Listening to a person, to the wind. Caressing a child. Scraping carrots in the sink. Weeping. Laughing.

Being tender. First I learned to be tender with myself; to tend the needs of my soul. Then I began to tend the *other* which is also my self. If I am not tending, caring for some small portion of the living creation, how can I commune with that creation, be it the earth or a child, in any but the most sentimental way? A woman learns, in caring for an infant, that she becomes bonded. A person who tends the land or gives to another discovers the same bond. These are not moral niceties, they are part of the mystery. They are *law*.

In this kind of communion with life, new languages arise in our bodies: languages of awe and wonder, gratitude and a joy that is overflowing. They soften us. And I wonder: are these the direction our human consciousness is taking? It seems a reciprocal process. The more gratitude or awe I feel, the more life shows forth its beauty *and* terror, the more my life is graced. These are the *languages of being*. Of *being alive*. This is a life lived with passion: com-passion.

We are called to a larger love. It hovers, dancing like a radiant field with the energies of our bodies. We bring our stories, each of us, to *that which leaves nothing out*. We bring the energies of our sorrow and our joy, our anger, grief and pain. We bring the energies of our fears, our despair, our hope. Our attention is vibrant with lives that are real. We tap that energy and are tuned finer. We bring who we are, our hearts and bodies and minds and souls. All of these we bring to the creative doorway of the unknown.

There we await the mystery.

So here we stand. If we are to live sacred lives, lives of meaning, we have to do the inner work. We have to bring our courage along with our fear. We learn to follow our images and metaphors. To trust the tender connection.

There is a magnet which draws us forward, and the journey has ways of confirming our every step. We tune to the subtle hints that help us along. We find our guides and our companions along the way.

We need each other. For even though we do our own work, this is no longer a personal spiritual journey. In the story of the universe, just as the time is over for the creation of oceans, so is it over for *individual* quests for enlightenment. We are on a broader path, the path of all life. And all of creation is on it.

So, when we feel most alone, we discover we are not. We realize we can never be lost. When it seems most dark, life discloses what we need. Help comes from the most surprising places. *The different way* appears suddenly right in front of us, whenever we look. We all find our own confirmation for the journey, just as I found meaning in the butterflies and the deer. We find our own rock at the bottom of the gorge and we stand on it. We come to the place where we always knew who we were.

Then we will become like streaming comets, blazing the path of who we have been into the tapestry of stories that is the universe.

Let this be our celebration of life together, for every moment of the journey is afire with mystery: every dream, every synchronicity, every poem; each creative thought and each event; the birth of compassion and the death of loved ones. We shall never understand; but we can hold to the real.

We look with uncertainty beyond the old choices for clear-cut answers to a softer, more permeable aliveness which is every moment at the brink of death; for something new is being born in us if we but let it. We stand at a new doorway, awaiting that which comes, trailing what may seem flimsy garments: a less defended posture, a willing stance, naked without our beliefs, our judgment. Daring to be human creatures. Vulnerable to the beauty of existence. Learning to love. Inquiring into the mystery.

Loving life.

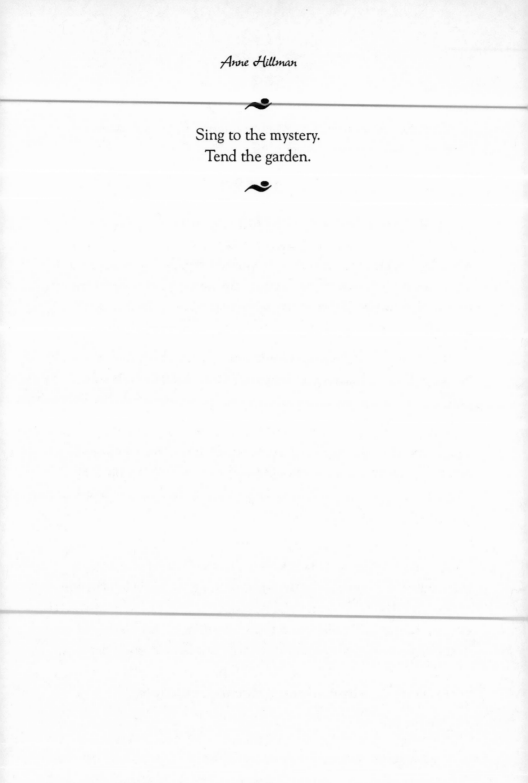

Sing to the mystery.
Tend the garden.

14

Coda: Belonging

He was probably two and a half. He had a shock of blond hair sticking straight out from under a baseball cap and wore an outlandish set of red rimmed sun glasses. He was walking barefoot across the small beach with his father, and as I caught his eye, I wiggled the fingers on my left hand in greeting. He ran towards me, talking nonstop, until he reached the weathered log where I sat a few feet from the ocean's edge. It was a monologue of introduction—not of himself, but of his immediate world: "The waves. High ones. Crash on the rocks!" He clapped his hands, mimicking the waves, then gestured to the far end of the beach. "All the shells. See? Lots 'n lots." He danced a brief shell dance around the glistening deposits on the sand and shouted, "The sand's hot here!" then jumped to the damp tide line and admired the holes his feet made, "Wo-o-o-o! Co-o-o-ld! Look at the dog jumpin'! We can jump way up in the sky!"

He clenched his fists and cocked his elbows, then jumped and landed a few feet away. A piece of damp seaweed caught his eye and he bent to touch it. "Yuck!" He leapt back in disgust. I held the rubbery leaf while he examined it more closely. Then he handed me a stone. "Throw it in the water," he commanded. I did and was delighted to see I could throw just far enough that it splashed in the surf. His throw fell short of the water, so he handed me another.

His name was Neil. We had known each other maybe five minutes when he reached up and grabbed my hand, calling me to go closer to the water with him. With a backward glance at his father and a joy I had forgotten, I accompanied him as far as he dared go: he stopped, dug his toes in the sand, afraid of the oncoming water. I tugged his hand and smiled, "C'mon, let's run up the beach!" and we pounded away from the shoreline together. Back and forth we ran until his attention was caught by something else he wanted me to do. I can still feel his soft small hand in mine, sandy, warm, gripping me tightly. I saw myself as a stranger but he did not. He knew he belonged.

I could feel his sense of belonging. It was as palpable as the stones he handed me to throw in the ocean. Like a spark, it rekindled that experience in me, the feeling of connectedness and trust, of really belonging to something larger. It was something subtle, like a promise lying just beneath my awareness; a promise of human community and more.

I remembered, too, how this sense of belonging always seems to arrive unexpectedly, often in moments of solitude.

One day in Oakland, I sat with a group of friends and asked them about their experiences of belonging. Although our stories were different, I felt a kinship with each person because of these deep kinds of common occurrences we had shared. Mary Ellen, a young teacher, was canoeing in the Quetico Provincial Park,

Ontario and bent, one morning, to dip her tin cup in the clear water for a drink. Time seemed to stop and she thought, *"This is all that matters,"* and, though the words didn't quite express it, *"I am rain, water, canoe, cup."* Jim, another friend, told a similar story: He was swimming in the ocean and suddenly knew the salt water to be *"like a poultice, a cleansing, drawing the chaos out of me."*

These awarenesses tend to arrive in moments when we are deep inside our bodies: stopping at the top of a hill after a long bicycle ride, pulling hard through a whitewater rapids, lying at a campsite under the stars. They come when we are moved by an experience in nature or by a story told by a friend. They often happen when our hearts are full. But they may not be full of happiness, as my story for the group that morning illustrates:

It was 1977. We had just buried my father. I went down to the beach on the Florida gulf at sunset to be still for a while. As I sat on the warm white sand, I scooped some up and let it sift through my fingers, looking at the pearly shells left in my palm, feeling my grief. After an indeterminable time, I sensed a movement out of the corner of my eye and looked up. There stood all around me at least twenty seagulls, facing toward me in a perfect circle. I could not believe what I was seeing, but I thought, *"I am cared for...I am not alone."*

Reflections of the inner journey such as these, are present in all of us. At times, something at the core of our being is touched and there is a healing. Boundaries unexpectedly dissolve and we feel sustained in our true identity. We know we are part of something larger.

Neil didn't *think* about this something larger. He *was* it. He didn't introduce himself as "I, Neil." He introduced the beach, the sky, the shells, the moment. He reached his hand up in trust because I was part of it too. I joined him as another child and knew the joy and the wonder of playing briefly outside time.

A mystic[1] once said "Life bubbles up out of the depths until it spills over." It spilled over in Neil. It spilled over in a tin cup, in an ocean swim and in a circle of birds. It spills over eternally.

Notes

Author's Preface

1. From Rainer Maria Rilke, untitled, from *The Selected Poetry of Rainer Maria Rilke*, edited and translated by Stephen Mitchell (New York: Random House, 1982), p. 261.

2. Morris Berman, *Coming to our Senses* (New York: Simon and Schuster, 1989), p. 344.

Prologue

1. Stanwood Cobb, Ed., *Patterns in Jade of Wu Ming Fu* (Washington: Avalon Press, 1935), as reprinted in *The Choice is Always Ours*, edited by Dorothy Berkley Phillips, Elizabeth Boyden Howes and Lucille M. Nixon (Wheaton, IL: ReQuest Books, The Theosophical Publishing House, 1975), P. 42. (Wu Ming Fu was a Chinese poet and philosopher).

Chapter One

1. Jean L. McKechnie, Ed., *Webster's Deluxe Unabridged Dictionary* (New York: Simon and Schuster, 1979), p. 953.

Chapter Two

1. James Gleick, "New Appreciation of the Complexity in a Flock of Birds," *The New York Times*, November 24, 1987.

2. Andrew Bard Schmookler, *Out of Weakness: Healing the Wounds That Drive Us to War* (Toronto: Bantam Books, 1988), p. 305. (Emphasis added.)

3. Thomas Berry, *The Dream of the Earth* (San Francisco: Sierra Club Books, 1988), pp. 42f. Berry has proposed the idea of the need for a larger, inclusive story for the human race.

4. The story of the autotrophs and prokaryotes is described variously by many authors, among them, Erich Jantsch in *The Self-Organizing Universe* (Oxford: Pergamon Press), 1980, pp. 109f; Sean McDonagh in *To Care for the Earth* (Santa Fe: Bear & Co., 1986), pp. 85f;

and unpublished works by Brian Swimme. For your further reference, see pp.88-92 in *The Universe Story* by Brian Swimme and Thomas Berry, just published by HarperSanFrancisco, 1992.

Chapter Three

1. Rainer Maria Rilke, "Archaic Torso of Apollo," *Selected Poetry of Rainer Maria Rilke*, edited and translated by Stephen Mitchell (New York: Random House, 1982), p. 61.

Chapter Four

1. James Hillman, *A Blue Fire* (New York: Harper and Row, 1989), p. 259.

Chapter Five

1. Fritz Kunkel, *In Search of Maturity* (New York: Charles Scribner's Sons, 1943), reprinted in Phillips et al, *The Choice Is Always Ours*, p. 105.

2. All of the poetry in this chapter was written in 1986.

3. Thomas Berry, *The Dream of the Earth* (San Francisco: Sierra Club Books, 1988), pp. viii, 14, 48, 64.

4. Brian Swimme, lecture, September, 1987.

Chapter Six

1. Gregory Bateson, *Mind and Nature* (New York: Bantam Books, 1980), pp. 12-13.

Chapter Seven

1. From an artwork entitled *"Fantastic"* by Louisa Jenkins, on loan from the private collection of Donna and Tom Ambrogi, San Francisco, to the Santa Sabina Center, San Rafael, CA.

2. "Hatred," 1986.

3. C.G. Jung, "Synchronicity: An Acausal Connecting Principle," in C.G. Jung and W. Pauli, *The Interpretation of Nature and the Psyche* (New York: Pantheon Books, 1955).

4. C. G. Jung, "Commentary," in Richard Wilhelm with C.G. Jung, *The Secret of the Golden Flower—a Chinese Book of Life* (New York: Harcourt Brace), 1962, p. 94. Quoted in Matthew Fox, *Original Blessing* (Santa Fe: Bear & Co., 1983), p. 198.

5. The ideas in this paragraph were developed by Brian Swimme in a lecture on Thomas Berry's Principle 3, "The Universe as a Psychic Reality," September, 1987.

Chapter Eight

1. Christopher Alexander, *The Timeless Way of Building* (New York: Oxford University Press, 1979), p. 15.

2. A case in point is that of Friedrich Kekule, whose image of a snake biting its tail led to his theory of the benzene ring.

3. Brain Swimme emphasizes the need for this kind of creativity. See also some of Richard Moss's works, particularly *An Inspired Life*, audiotape (Bandera, TX: Richard Moss Seminars, 1988).

4. Brian Swimme's phrase from a lecture in 1987 is a beautiful expression of an abandonment etched deeply in the human soul.

5. See Matthew Fox, *Original Blessing*, pp. 132f, in which he summarizes traditions and poets of East and West on the subject.

6. Matthew Fox, *A Spirituality Named Compassion* (Minneapolis: Winston Press, 1979), pp. 254-255. Fox credits William James with the second phrase.

7. Matthew Fox, *A Spirituality Named Compassion*, p. 257.

8. Shamanic lore has been extensively researched by scholars such as Carlos Casteneda and the noted anthropologist Michael Harner.

9. The leaders, Brenda and Michael Donahoe, now of Zephyr Cove, Nevada, are Organizational Development consultants, and have been apprenticed to Michael Harner.

10. Jeremy Taylor, *Dream Work* (New York: Paulist Press, 1983), p. 166.

11. Terms coined respectively by Jeremy Taylor and Bea Ledyard, an Associate with Richard Moss.

12. Jeremy Taylor cites supportive research in *Dream Work*, p. 6.

13. The Book of Job, 42:3, *Jerusalem Bible* translation.

Chapter Nine

1. Jacob Needleman, public lecture, San Francisco, 1988.

Chapter Ten

1. Sources for the Story are all antecedent to the magnificent new *The Universe Story* by Brian Swimme and Thomas Berry. My sources include:

> Brian Swimme, lectures, fall, 1987.
> Brian Swimme, *The Universe Is A Green Dragon* (Santa Fe: Bear & Co., 1984), (entire).

Thomas Berry, lectures and conversations, fall 1987 and spring, 1988, in Oakland and San Rafael, CA.
Sean McDonough, *To Care for the Earth*, pp. 77-103.
Patricia Mische, lecture, Oakland, CA, February 1988.
Loren Eiseley, *The Immense Journey* (New York: Vintage Books, 1946), pp. 61-77.

2. This is the opinion of Patricia Mische as well as several other sources for the Cosmic Story cited in the first footnote of the chapter.

Chapter Eleven

1. "Grief and the Heart," 1988.

2. "The Void," 1986.

3. Brian Swimme, lecture, fall, 1987 (On Allurement).

4. Nel Noddings, *Caring, A Feminine Approach to Ethics and Moral Education* (Berkeley and Los Angeles: University of California Press, 1984). See also Carol Gilligan, *In A Different Voice, Psychological Theory and Women's Development* (Cambridge MA: Harvard University Press, 1982).

5. Meister Eckhart's term. In *Breakthrough, Meister Eckhart's Creation Spirituality in New Translation*, Introduction and Commentaries by Matthew Fox (Garden City, N.Y: Image Books, 1980).

6. Gregory Bateson, public lecture, Berkeley, CA, 1978.

Chapter Twelve

1. Albert Einstein, "What I Believe," in *Out of My Later Years* (London: Thames & Hudson, 1950), 123.

2. "Loneliness," 1970.

3. Nikos Kazantzakis, *The Saviors of God: Spiritual Exercises*, translated by Kimon Friar (New York: Simon and Schuster, 1960), pp. 63, 78, 79. Original translation reads "...the work of man..."

4. Years ago I read these words of an age-old mystic, but I cannot find the source.

5. "Kin," from *Sierra Poems*, 1990.

6. "Grass," 1982.

7. Rainer Maria Rilke, "Sonnets to Orpheus" II, 14, in *Selected Poetry of Rainer Maria Rilke*, edited and translated by Stephen Mitchell (New York: Random House, 1982), p. 247.

8. "Rainforest Dawn," April, 1991.

9. "On the Edge," from *Sierra Poems*, 1990.

10. Richard Moss asks if perhaps families are breaking up because they can't train for the new consciousness. *Living with Paradox*, audiotape (Bandera, TX: Richard Moss Seminars, 1985).

11. Brian Swimme, lecture, 1987.

12. God's answer to Moses when Moses asked His name. It is a statement of *being*. Exodus 3:14.

13. Richard Moss.

14. Psalm 42, *New Revised Standard Version*.

Chapter Thirteen

1. Ram Dass, lecture.

2. Stephen Mitchell, *The Gospel According to Jesus, A New Translation and Guide To His Essential Teachings For Believers and Unbelievers* (New York: Harper Collins, Publishers, 1991), p. 12.

3. "Unknowing," 1990.

4 Richard Moss discussing more on the great commandments in *Love Is The Teacher*, audiotape (Bandera, TX: Richard Moss Seminars, 1983).

5 Richard Moss. *Love Is The Teacher*.

Chapter Fourteen

1. Meister Eckhart (c. 1260-c. 1329), quoted by Matthew Fox in *Breakthrough, Meister Eckhart's Creation Spirituality in New Translation*.

The Author

As an Organizational Development consultant for twenty years, Anne Hillman, M.Ed., functioned as a change agent for hospitals, businesses, schools, government and non-profit organizations throughout the United States, helping individuals and work groups to initiate their own growth and development in times of rapid change. Working with senior management and their entire organizations, she assisted her clients to shed preconceived ideas and forms in order to tap new levels of group functioning and creativity. Since 1978, her own creative work has led to an inquiry into the internal aspects of social change—reaching beyond psychology and traditional institutional approaches. After studying with Brian Swimme and Thomas Berry, she has focused on the interior human development required to support their work. She is certified by ICCS, a graduate Institute in Creation Spirituality founded by Matthew Fox, and in Ontological Studies by Richard Moss, M.D.